Remodeling & Decorating
Bedrooms

By the Editors of Sunset Books and Sunset Magazine

LANE PUBLISHING CO.,
Menlo Park, California

Begin and end your day in a better bedroom

If your bedroom's been sleeping through your remodeling and redecorating projects, now's the time to awaken its potential. In this book we've put together down-to-earth information and star-studded photographs to help you bring about your dream room.

Floor plans are included to explain certain concepts; they are drawn to varying scales.

Many people generously contributed ideas and information for this book. We'd like to thank Nancy Hewitt Clarke, Jean and Nate Kraft, Robyn Shotwell Metcalf, Michael Moyer, Don Mullen, Richard Pennington, The Right Touch, Pam Seifert, Linda J. Selden, and Kathy Strauss, as well as all the architects, designers, and homeowners who shared their bedroom design projects with us.

Edited by
Maureen Williams Zimmerman

Staff Editor:
Kathryn L. Arthurs

Special Consultants:
Hilary Hannon
Donald W. Vandervort

Design:
Antonia Manganaro

Illustrations:
Mark Pechenik, AIA

Cover: Inviting window seat and flower-bedecked fireplace make this bedroom special. Sweep of carpeting and warm orange print on window seat and bedspread add to cozy feeling. (Also see page 27.) *Architects:* Fisher-Friedman Associates. *Interior Designer:* Randee Seiger. *Photograph:* Jack McDowell.

Sunset Books
Editor, David E. Clark
Managing Editor, Elizabeth L. Hogan

Third printing March 1988

CONTENTS

Getting Started   4

Vacation cabin or multistory mansion,
every house has a bedroom or two

Small Bedrooms & Guest Rooms   14

For a guest or for yourself,
tuck a bed into a tight corner

Bedroom Offices & Sewing Places   24

In the bedroom's peace and quiet,
stitch a seam or review a report

Bedroom Sitting Areas   32

For a place to chat, take tea,
or just doze by the fire

Bed & Bath Combinations   40

For sounder sleeping and better bathing,
ally the house's two private rooms

Bedroom Decks, Windows & Skylights   48

Open the bedroom to starlight, fresh air,
and early morning dew

Ideas for Bedroom Lighting   56

Let the lights gleam, glint, and glow
after the sun goes down

Bedside Amenities   64

Around the bed: Stack bedtime stories,
tune in late-night TV, unwind with music

Dressing Rooms & Closets   72

Tubs, bins, baskets, and drawers
to keep your clothes composed

Index   80

Bedroom Furniture to Build

Headboard cabinet has a slanting backrest   23
Slanting side tables to add to your bed   31
Triangular headboard fits into a corner   39
Platform bed puts you on a pedestal   47
Bedside boxes stack high or low   55
Lights bridge the head of the bed   63
Water bed frame features compartments   71
Organizer: in a closet or on its own   79

Getting Started

*Vacation cabin or multistory mansion,
every house has a bedroom or two*

At its simplest, a bedroom is nothing but a room with a bed in it. At its most sumptuous, a bedroom can be a veritable second house within the main house. On the spectrum of styles, most of us favor something in between Waldenesque simplicity and a bedroom fit for Mad King Ludwig's Bavarian castle. But even within the middle range of styles, you'll find a wealth of choices for remodeling, redecorating, or designing a bedroom.

You may choose a small, cozy sleeping chamber or spacious lounging quarters. Depending on temperament, you may prefer a bright, up-with-the-birds room or a dark den for long hibernation. You may want to merge office space or sewing space with your bedroom. Or you may want your bedroom to double as a private retreat where you can read, listen to music, watch television, or—in Thackeray's phrase—"lead a life of dignified otiosity," sipping champagne in bed while eating Beluga caviar on toast points.

The first phase in planning is to know what kind of bedroom suits you. You may have a clear picture of the perfect room for you and want to browse through this book for solutions to practical problems. Or you may want to gain an idea here and an idea there as you look through the book, gradually working toward a plan that is yours alone. The bedroom that gives you sweet dreams may give another person nightmares, but you might as well customize your bedroom to suit yourself. After all, the cliché is true—you do spend a third of your life there.

An integral part of the house

A bedroom's location influences the type of room it is. If you desire a bedroom retreat, there's no point locating it in the middle of your home's high-traffic pattern. You'd be better off with a satellite room, connected by a walkway to the living and eating areas. At the other extreme, you may prefer a central bedroom tucked into the interior of the house.

Location also can affect how cool or warm a bedroom stays—not to mention how quiet or noisy it is.

The critical link between the bedroom and such specific other rooms as the bathroom (pages 40–46) and the dressing room (pages 72–78) is discussed in depth in special sections of this book. On pages 24–38 you'll find information on expanding the uses of the bedroom beyond sleeping—so it becomes several rooms in one. There are even ideas on conserving energy (page 6) and a section on relating the bedroom to the outdoors (pages 48–54).

Public/private areas of the house

Separation of one or more bedrooms from the rest of the house is a fine idea, space permitting. Many people think of the bedroom area as a retreat, a place to keep private. The farther the bedrooms are from the parts of the house where family and guests collect, the better.

The front door and entry hall are public; certainly the living room and dining room are, and sometimes the family room and kitchen. Separating the bedrooms from these areas will promote peace and quiet.

If one side of the house is right on the street or too close to neighbors, that side counts as a "public" part of the house, also, in your planning.

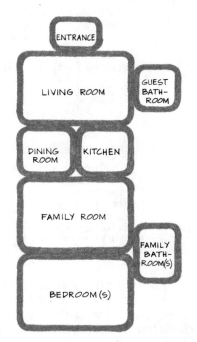

TO PRESERVE PRIVACY, you may want to locate the bedrooms as far as possible from the entrance to the house.

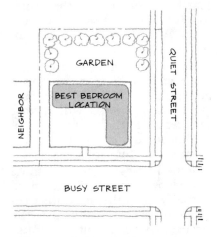

LOTS OF ACTIVITY outside can create noise. Consider the surroundings before finalizing location.

Of course, there are some bedrooms that needn't be separated from the more public parts of the house, and even some that shouldn't be. If a bedroom is doubling as a home office, for example, it may be convenient to have it close to the public areas. If the house belongs to just one person or to a two-person family, privacy may not be an important consideration, and a loft bedroom that's open to the rest of the house may be convenient.

Upstairs/downstairs

Any house with more than one level—be it a one-story with a basement or a three-story with an attic—presents a variety of possible bedroom configurations.

In a typical two-story house, most often the bedrooms are upstairs and the living areas downstairs. But this arrangement can be reversed. If, for example, there's a great view from the second story, the bedrooms might well be downstairs and the living room and kitchen upstairs. Or the bedrooms could be distributed on more than one level. Sometimes a bedroom loft can fit between levels.

In a three-level house, the rooms could be divided up to form a living level, a master bedroom level, and a secondary bedrooms level.

Split-level houses tend to have one or more bedrooms downstairs, and sometimes an extra bedroom is built in a basement. Providing good lighting on a lower level can be a challenge since natural light may come from one di-

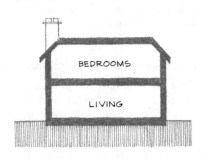

TYPICAL TWO-STORY HOUSE has bedrooms upstairs and the rest of the living quarters downstairs.

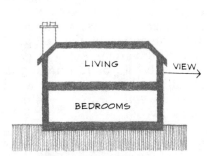

IF YOU DON'T MIND daytime stair climbing, take advantage of a view by putting the living areas upstairs.

rection only or from small high-up window slits. Basements can be damp, too. Still, downstairs bedrooms are usually cool and quiet; in fact, some auxiliary heating may be needed during cold weather.

Attic conversion is one way to acquire additional bedroom space. Conversion is most feasible if the attic already has enough headroom (7½ feet over at least half of the usable floor area); raising the roof is expensive and can be tricky structurally. Finishing the attic floor is relatively easy if the foundation, bearing walls, and existing attic floor joists are adequate. Since attics can be too hot in summer and too cold in winter, adequate insulation and cross-ventilation are extremely important. One positive aspect of attic conversions is sometimes mistaken for a negative: the space is often irregularly shaped, with changing ceiling heights. These circumstances offer novel room shape possibilities and space under the eaves that can be an asset, not a head-bumping liability.

(Continued on next page)

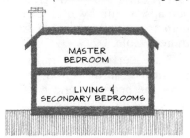

ANOTHER POSSIBILITY in a multilevel house: divide the bedrooms among two or more floors.

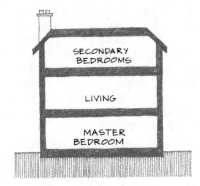

WITH MORE THAN TWO FLOORS, the number of options for bedroom location increases.

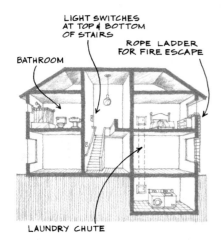

LIGHT SWITCHES AT TOP & BOTTOM OF STAIRS

ROPE LADDER FOR FIRE ESCAPE

BATHROOM

LAUNDRY CHUTE

UPPER-STORY BEDROOMS can benefit from features such as those indicated in this drawing.

. . . Upstairs/downstairs (cont'd.)

Whichever floor you choose for a bedroom, it's best to have a bathroom on the same level. And there are other considerations to plan for: You'll want light switches at both the top and bottom of the stairs so you don't have to climb stairs in the dark. On upper stories, consider fire safety—be sure to have a practical exit in mind. A laundry chute and perhaps a dumbwaiter can also help to make upstairs bedrooms more livable.

Older persons and those with physical disabilities may prefer to have the bedroom and bathroom on the same level as the living area.

The wing idea

If the master bedroom is separated from the rest of the bedrooms, it becomes an "adult wing." Such a wing may be a bedroom suite complete with separate bathroom and sitting room or study. A children's wing may have its own bathroom and play room. In some houses, the adult wing is next to the living room, and the children's bedrooms adjoin the family room.

For more separation, the parents' bedroom can be on a different floor than the children's bedrooms.

Parents often want a baby's nursery close to their bedroom.

But as children grow, bedroom arrangements often change. One architect suggests you "allow 10 feet for every year." But the rooms should be located so that when children leave home, their bedrooms can be converted for other uses, such as a crafts room, office, or guest bedroom.

PLAYROOM

CHILD'S BEDROOM

BATH

CHILD'S BEDROOM

BATH STUDY

MASTER BEDROOM

BUFFERED by the rest of the house are these separate sleeping quarters and baths for adults and children.

Planning for energy efficiency

When it comes to planning a house that's energy efficient, each room can be considered separately. Here we discuss making the bedroom less expensive to heat and cool within the context of the rest of the house.

On pages 48–54 you'll find information on relating the bedroom to the out-of-doors—designing landscaping to conserve energy, taking into account the advantages and disadvantages of different points of the compass, and using various kinds of glass effectively. If you're thinking of installing a fireplace or a wood stove in your bedroom, turn to pages 33–34.

A bedroom's temperature can be different from that of the rest of the house. If you use the bedroom only for sleeping snugly under warm blankets, you can keep

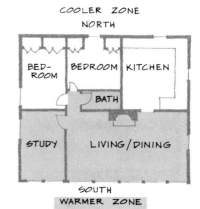

COOLER ZONE
NORTH

BED-ROOM BEDROOM KITCHEN

BATH

STUDY LIVING/DINING

SOUTH
WARMER ZONE

CONSERVE ENERGY by grouping the bedrooms with other rooms you keep cooler than the rest of the house.

it quite cool all the time. If you use the bedroom as an office or sitting room during the day, you could heat it during the day only.

A new house or a house undergoing major remodeling can be divided into temperature zones, with the rooms that need warmth together in one part of the house, rooms that should be cooler in another. A bedroom may well be in the cool section.

Doors between the bedroom and the rest of a temperature-zoned house must close tightly. Insulated interior walls will further seal heat into the warmer part of the house; they can make the bedroom stuffy, though.

Some houses—especially those heated by direct sunlight—have virtually no walls or barriers between rooms. In such houses, the arrangement of rooms moderates the temperature. Bedrooms in these houses are often placed in an upper story or loft so that downstairs heat simply filters up to them (see example on page 35).

HEAT MOVES EASILY THROUGH OPEN LOFT

The bed—the reason for the room

The most important decisions in bedroom planning involve the bed: the kind of bed to use and where to put it. Some types of beds are built in. Others, though they are freestanding pieces of furniture, are large and imposing. In a well-designed bedroom, the bed's logical location is usually obvious even when there's not a stick of furniture in the room.

Since 8 hours or more of the time spent in the bedroom is spent in or on the bed, you should use the bed as the room design's starting point. For example, the view *from* the bed is more important than the view *of* the bed. Traffic patterns begin and end at the bed, and the location of satellite areas, such as clothing storage or a place to comb your hair, will evolve from the bed's placement.

Types of beds

What is and is not customary, comfortable, and convenient for sleeping depends on where in the world you live. In Japan, you unfold a *futon* (a cushiony sleeping mat) at night, then store it at dawn. In the South Pacific, you retire to a hammock. Each of these beds is both practical and comfortable, especially for people who've grown up with them.

The Western bed tends to be less portable. In Europe, the bed was for many centuries a prized status symbol—the most important piece of furniture in the house. Its size reflected its importance: the 16th century Great Bed of Ware measured 10 feet 11 inches square.

In this section we discuss various types of beds from A to W—from adjustable beds to water beds. If you need to make the most of limited floor space in your bedroom, if you need sitting space, or if you're planning a guest room, a part-time bed may be the answer. In addition to futons and hammocks, consider the ideas on pages 14–22 for small-space beds and guest beds.

Adjustable beds and hospital beds.

People have found after hospital stays that the beds they used there, with adjustable head and foot, are fun to have at home for sitting up to read, write, or watch television.

ADJUSTABLE BED bends at both the head and the foot so you can change the angles to suit you.

Furniture outlets often carry adjustable beds, modifications of hospital beds. These usually bend at the head and foot but don't elevate. Sometimes they're sold in a package with a bolted-together box spring, mattress, frame, and mechanism. Often the beds are electrically operated, but you may be able to find a hand-crank model. Vibrating motors are available as an option with some adjustable beds.

The original model—the bed used in hospitals—can also be purchased. Try hospital supply outlets. Some retailers of hospital beds will sell the bed components—springs, frame, mattress, and mechanism—separately.

Antique beds. Guidelines for choosing an antique bed are generally the same as those for choosing any other antique. Libraries are full of books on antiques; experience in shopping is an excellent teacher, too.

An antique bed might be your choice for a number of reasons: its style or uniqueness, the quality of its construction, sentimental value, or its worth as a possession of increasing value.

Perhaps the most important consideration in choosing an antique bed is its usability: will it be comfortable to sleep on? Its size—height as well as width and length—may be quite different from present uniform bed dimensions if it is more than 150 years old. Even beds less than 150 years old will usually be higher than today's typical bed if you set a box spring and mattress on the existing bed frame. Some people like a higher bed; if you don't, you could dispense with the box spring (see page 11).

You'll need to check the frame for ease in installing a mattress. Both bolted metal mattress rails and wooden mattress rails can be moved to accommodate a standard mattress. With some very old beds it may be necessary to build mattress supports into the frame. Innerspring mattresses can be custom-made or a foam mattress cut to fit.

Altering, repairing, and refinishing an antique bed involves many of the same considerations that apply to any antique. A damaged bed will cost considerably less than one in good condition, and a bed that you alter may not have the value of an antique in good, mostly original condition. An antique dealer can probably direct you to someone for repair and refinishing; for do-it-yourself

CALLED A SLEIGH BED, this antique is an Americanized version of Empire style; it's attractive from any angle.

help, see the *Sunset* book *Furniture Finishing & Refinishing*.

In general terms, bedroom furniture made prior to the Queen Anne period is quite scarce. Eighteenth century beds in Queen Anne, Georgian, Chippendale, or Hepplewhite style are slightly more available; Sheraton, Directoire, and Empire designs are more commonly found. You're most likely to come across rope or spool-turned beds from the Victorian era. Some of these wood beds were made with matching chests and dressers.

Antique wicker day beds and headboards can be found. Day beds are a bit narrow for comfortable sleeping, though they may be all right for a child or a surplus of guests. Also, unless you really prefer an antique, consider new wicker headboards, which are in abundant supply. Repaired wicker won't last long unless it has been fixed correctly, so you'll want to locate an experienced person to make repairs; better still, find a piece in excellent condition.

Wicker can be stripped of paint by a furniture refinisher—doing it yourself would be a tedious job. Use a spray device for a freshly painted look, or leave the wicker natural.

Following is information on metal beds and canopy beds, both popular types that are available as antiques, as well as new styles.

Brass and other metal. Metal bedsteads became common in the second half of the 19th century. Rolled steel and cast iron beds with ornamental brass joints were popular, as were bed frames of brass-wrapped steel tubing. Very few solid brass beds were made—solid brass is quite heavy and not as strong as steel.

To refurbish an iron or steel frame, have it sandblasted to remove paint and rust, then paint it yourself or have it enameled. Solid

Here's a bevy of beds

SPOOL BED was a favorite with the Victorians; many examples are still to be found in antique shops.

MOCK CANOPY BED—its canopy suspended from the ceiling instead of from the bed frame—copies a classic.

FLOATING EFFECT of a pedestal-style platform bed suits a small bedroom— bed appears to take up little space.

BRIGHT AND SHINY brass bed, whether antique or contemporary, adds sparkle to any bedroom.

CONTEMPORARY CANOPY BED is a fresh variation on an ancient theme. Modern materials lend sleekness.

ON THIRD LEVEL is a platform bed. Platform extension at the foot of the bed substitutes for a table.

brass parts and brass-clad metal tubing should be polished professionally—it's a difficult and time-consuming process to attempt yourself. If the brass coating is torn or ripped, you could search for a replacement piece, though an exact duplicate may be difficult to find.

Most brass beds manufactured currently are protected against tarnishing and scratching. King-size frames are available in brass.

Canopy beds. Descendants of the canopied, curtained beds of medieval castles are still with us, both in re-creations of the originals and in restyled, modernized versions. The great appeal of a canopy bed is its room-within-a-room ambience—it provides a cozy, enclosed space. The drawback to a canopy bed is its size, real and apparent. These beds often require a high ceiling and can overwhelm a small room.

In its simplest form, a canopy bed can be created by fabric or other material suspended from the ceiling above the bed or from one or more walls. A fabric canopy could be draped into loose billows, shirred between rods, or pulled taut. A panel of heavy cardboard or lightweight wood could be painted or otherwise decorated to serve as a canopy. If you choose a suspended canopy (thus dispensing with bedposts), be sure the canopy is anchored securely to ceiling or wall joists.

Today, bed frames complete with bedposts and canopy come in many styles and materials, from graceful metal to geometric rattan or carved wood. Sometimes the bed has a solid headboard reaching all the way to the canopy.

Other canopy frameworks are simply supports to drape fabric over. Fabric often embellishes canopy beds in the form of lining, valances, curtains, and draperies. Lacy eyelet or netting lightens the appearance of a large canopy bed; heavier fabrics give a snug feeling and can even serve their original purpose—shutting out drafts.

Pedestal-style platform beds. If the section of the bed frame underneath the mattress is smaller than the mattress, it looks like a pedestal. Useful in a small room, this type of bed seems visually to take up less space than most other styles of bed. Sometimes there is simply an indentation (like a kitchen toe space) at the base of the bed frame, giving the bed a floating effect.

Photographs showing pedestal-style platform beds are on pages 36 and 54.

Platform beds. This style of bed has a wonderfully streamlined look. A platform bed is raised one or more steps up from floor level, and it may have storage built in. Such a bed is especially effective in a bedroom having more than one floor level, where it can eliminate the need for some furniture pieces. Check to see if the local building code strictly limits the floor area over which you can reduce ceiling height, though.

Whether you decide on a built-in platform or a movable one nailed together out of plywood, it can be surfaced with wood, tile, or carpeting to match or contrast with the floor material. Carpeting or upholstering makes the platform more comfortable to sit on or lean against.

Because a mattress usually sits directly on the platform instead of on a box spring, a platform bed is often firmer and lower than most people are used to. Sometimes the top of the mattress and the surface of the platform are on one plane.

For examples of platform beds, see the photographs on pages 19, 22, 29, and 53.

Another use of the term "platform" refers to a high, loftlike structure reached by a ladder or stairs. Such a structure can save space dramatically in a high-ceilinged room. We discuss platform-type lofts in the section on small bedrooms on page 18.

Vibrating beds. Vibrator mechanisms come as standard equipment on some models of electric adjustable beds. They're also available as separate electric units that attach to the wooden frame of a box spring. Some vibrating units offer several speeds; some shut off automatically after a certain length of time.

Water beds. Water bed design has taken great steps forward since the 1960s. Newer water mattresses come with a solidly comfortable foam edge; others use an air baffle or rows of springs along the mattress perimeter, and baffles of various designs inside some mattresses slow down wave motion.

These new mattress designs have made new, more streamlined frame designs possible. They look so much like typical box spring and mattress sets that they're called "hybrid water beds," and you can't tell that they're water beds until you test them. (These beds are not interchangeable with standard bed components, though. The frame, for example, has extra legs and is reinforced to support the weight of the water mattress.)

Mattress sizes vary from crib to larger than the standard king. Be sure to fit the mattress to the correct-size frame, especially if you're planning to use a vinyl bag-style mattress without a built-in perimeter. UL-approved heaters slide underneath the mattress.

Between the water mattress and the frame goes a polyurethane liner that contains the water in case of a leak. Using a liner is important—leaks can cause serious damage.

Newer water beds used with liners carry long-term guarantees against leaks. However, if the bed does spring a leak, the damage can be considerable. Replacing a hardwood floor or a prized rug isn't fun, even if your homeowner's insurance policy covers the damage to your property.

Frames for water beds offer a wide choice. A box of pine 2 by 10s that sits right on the floor can be used, of course, but you can also find sleek hardwood frames. Monolithic wood frames offer cabinetry underneath and a wooden canopy overhead. With

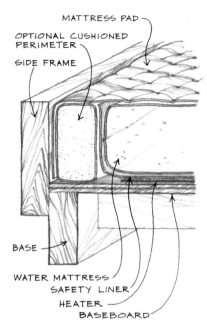

ANATOMY OF A WATER BED: *Perimeter of foam, air, or springs is an option that makes the bed comfortable.*

many frame styles, drawers can be added as an option. You can also add cushioned side rails. On page 71 you'll see a water bed frame to build yourself.

You needn't worry about the weight of the water bed if your house is constructed according to current building codes. Depending on the depth of the mattress and the way in which the weight of the bed is directed onto the floor, a water bed applies less pressure per square foot than a grand piano, refrigerator, or bathtub. If yours is an older house, you could obtain the specifications of your bed from the manufacturer and check them with your community building department. If you're still in doubt, consult a structural engineer to determine the floor's bearing capacity.

Underneath it all: The mattress & foundation

Though the style of your bed sets the tone for the look of your bedroom, it's the mattress and its foundation that have the most to do with how comfortably you sleep.

Basically, the choices are few: you're likely to have either a foam

mattress or an innerspring mattress. The mattress, in turn, must rest on some sort of foundation—often, though not necessarily, a box spring. And all of that will rest on some sort of bed frame or on a flat surface.

Foam mattresses. If you want to refurbish an antique bed or if you have minimal money to spend, consider using a foam mattress. Foam is very resilient, yet it conforms to body shape. (Some doctors, in fact, recommend foam mattresses for people with back problems.) It can be custom-cut to

TRUNDLED OUT OF A TIGHT SPOT, *foam mattress fits where a spring mattress couldn't.*

fit an odd-size bed. The main drawback of a foam mattress is its warmth; it doesn't breathe like a spring mattress.

High-quality polyurethane foam is fire retardant, mildewproof, nonallergenic, and dry-cleanable. Guarantees run for 10 to 15 years. Foam's rate of return from compression is one measure of quality; the dealer can help you interpret the rate.

To be comfortable, a foam mattress should be at least 4 inches thick. Use a thicker mattress—about 6 inches thick—if the foam is not top quality or

if a very large person will be using the mattress.

To prolong the life of a foam mattress, cover it with a fabric case made of muslin or cotton ticking. A removable fabric case is easy to clean and protects the foam.

Turn a foam mattress frequently, especially if it rests on the floor or on a sheet of plywood. A frame with slats or with drilled ventilation holes is extra insurance against mildew.

In some parts of the country, mattress-size pieces of foam are hard to find. If you have trouble, try contacting an upholsterer or look in the Yellow Pages of a nearby city's telephone book under "Rubber—Foam & Sponge."

Innerspring mattresses. Outlets where these mattresses are sold usually display cut-away examples and provide literature to help you in your selection. Innerspring mattresses have springs connected in various ways and edges reinforced with steel bands, rods, or wires. Quality varies; let the

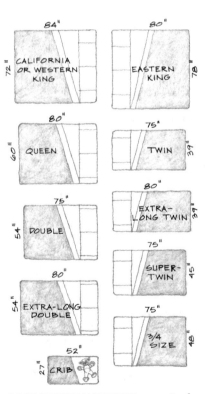

INNERSPRING MATTRESSES *come in these sizes. You can special-order other dimensions you require.*

length of the warranty guide you. Innerspring mattresses can be used on many different kinds of bases and frames.

It's best to actually test innerspring mattresses before you buy. You may want to visit the mattress department during hours when stores are least crowded, such as just after opening or during dinner hours. Stretch out on each mattress you're considering, to see if it would be comfortable for you. Take your time and don't worry about feeling foolish as you test mattresses—you want to make the right choice.

Be sure to follow the manufacturer's instructions for caring for your new mattress—particularly for turning it frequently during the first months of use.

Odd-size innerspring mattresses can be made for you; check with a local retailer.

Box springs and mattress bases. As a rule of thumb, the more solid the base, the longer the life of the mattress.

A simple sheet of plywood, or even the floor, makes an adequate mattress support. There is some chance of mildew if air cannot circulate underneath the mattress, but most mattress manufacturers discount this possibility. The advantages of a box spring or other mattress base are additional flexibility—springiness—of the mattress, and change in height.

Box springs are designed to be used as foundations for innerspring mattresses. For less height, you could try a pallet—a padded wooden mattress support often used for bunkbeds. A wooden slat support or a heavy canvas deck with cross wires underneath can also function as a mattress base.

Steel bed frames. Standard steel frames are often used with box spring and mattress sets. For a large bed—bigger than a double bed—be sure to use a strong frame, one with extra legs and cross bracing. Frames tend to spread with use. Casters, flat glides, or barrel-shaped rollers allow you to move the bed around, but they all leave marks on the rug.

Attaching headboards to bed frames

Many brass and wooden beds are constructed as one unit: headboard, footboard, and side rails all fit together. Most steel bed frames, on the other hand, are purchased separately from headboards. A separate, freestanding headboard can be used, or you can connect a headboard to the frame. (Wicker or rattan headboards are too fragile to be attached to a metal frame—they could be fastened to the wall instead.)

Most better-quality steel bed frames have headboard-attachment brackets welded or riveted to the frame. The headboard is bolted to the bed frame through predrilled holes in the brackets.

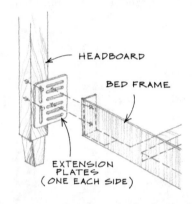

EXTENSION PLATES form bridge between frame and headboard when the headboard is wider than the bed frame.

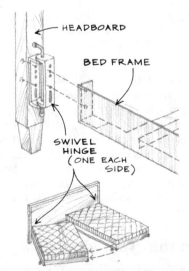

HEAVY HEADBOARD stays put while the bed frame—attached with swivel hinges—moves sideways.

With bed frames that have no attachment brackets, you can use an adapter plate (see information following) to attach the headboard.

For special headboard situations, many different plates are available. All plates come with bolts, nuts, and lockwashers (the long bolts go between plate and headboard, the shorter bolts between plate and frame).

Extension plates are used when the headboard is wider than the bed frame. For example, most wooden headboards are made for Eastern king-size beds and you'll need to use an extension plate if your bed is Western king-size.

Adapter plates are for frames that have no headboard-attachment brackets. They are metal angle brackets that bolt onto the bed frame and onto the headboard.

Swivel hinges allow you to attach two twin beds to a single

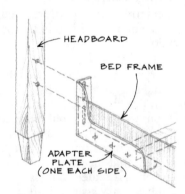

USE ADAPTER PLATES when the steel frame has no headboard-attachment brackets. Plates bolt to frame.

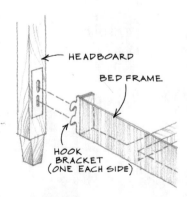

IF HEADBOARD has metal slots, attach the steel bed frame to it with a pair of these hook brackets.

king-size headboard or to move a corner-fitting bed easily when the headboard is stationary. With swivel hinges you can easily separate the beds while you make them.

Hook brackets are designed to be used with headboards and footboards that have steel slots into which hook brackets slide. The hook brackets bolt to the bed.

Placement of the bed

Beds can be freestanding, positioned with one end or side against a wall, or tucked into a corner or a special niche. Opinions vary on how much clearance is necessary around a bed, but 3 feet between the bed and a wall or other vertical surface seems reasonable. Two feet between a bed and another low surface—such as another bed—allows minimum room to stand and make the bed. Where a door swings outward or a drawer pulls open, be sure to leave extra clearance.

Especially with a platform bed, clearance above the bed is important. Four feet of headroom is the minimum for sitting upright.

The type of bed linens you use may make a difference in where you can put the bed. If you toss a quilt on top of a fitted bottom sheet, difficulty in bed-making will be inconsequential. But a bedspread that needs neat tucking-in on all sides means you should have easy access to all sides of the bed—so a freestanding bed

BED ALCOVE generates a feeling of privacy, neatly solves the problem of where to put the bed.

The view from the bed

LOTS TO LOOK AT and enjoy can personalize a bedroom; fireplace, sofa, and corner shelves lend warmth here.

OVERHEAD, you see a one-of-a-kind ceiling; to the side, mirrors reflect and enlarge the bedroom.

may be the most practical idea.

The design of the rest of the bedroom and related spaces depends on where you put the bed. See the next section, "Putting your ideas on paper," for planning help. If you have very little bedroom square footage, turn to "Small Bedrooms & Guest Rooms," pages 14–22.

Putting your ideas on paper

Once you've decided what you want from a bedroom design, or what problems you want solved

LINE OF VISION takes you out over the water while you're nestled snug in a curtained and canopied bed.

DYNAMIC FOCAL POINT—such as a large painting—dominates the view from the bed in a clutterless bedroom.

in a redesign, then you're ready to tackle the project.

Professional designers can give you answers to your questions of organization and style. These people are trained to think in three dimensions, and you'll find their help invaluable. Use an architect if structural changes are called for, an interior designer for alterations within an existing room. The cost of using a professional designer is often a very small percentage of the expense of materials and labor, and it pays dividends in your satisfaction with the results.

Whether or not you work with a professional, rough sketches, clippings, and sample floor plans are all useful tools. Be sure to think through what it is in a clipping that appeals to you, and whether the ideas really are applicable to the way you live. Remember that the whole room must be thought out, down to the smallest details, before you begin work. If you're experimenting with floor plans, don't neglect elevation drawings—these show the vertical elements in a room.

If you're planning structural changes, working drawings and a precise specifications list are essential. The results that could come from using rough sketches might rudely surprise and disappoint you, and playing it by ear can be extremely expensive.

Floor plans & sketches

At first, don't struggle with scale drawings on graph paper. Such drawings should be used to finalize your ideas, not to develop them. Meanwhile, even if your fourth grade teacher shook her head over your artistic ability, go ahead and sketch your ideas—you'll be able to clarify and communicate them much better than if you just talked about them.

Using the bed as your starting point, test your floor plan ideas. Try drawing lines for the paths you'll take from one part of the room to another. What will your morning pattern be? How can you avoid retracing your steps? Without putting obstacles in your path, how can you make the most of seemingly wasted expanses of floor space? What's the most direct route to the bathroom? The closet? Where will you sit to put on your shoes?

Try to imagine yourself in the room. From the bed, what will you see? Will you have enough privacy? Will morning light waken you gently, or glare into your eyes? Will there be drafts? Can you reach a light switch? Is there space for a television set? Where will you put a book and your glasses? Where are the windows and doors? What's the ceiling like?

Go through the rest of this book. Let the discussion of design considerations and the photographs of thoughtfully done bedrooms help you develop your plans. Then finalize your ideas by using to-scale graph paper drawings. Furniture templates will help you plan room arrangements. Templates are available in art supply stores, or you can measure your own furniture and cut out to-scale templates from cardboard or paper.

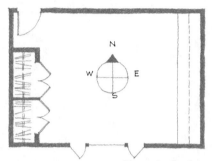

INTERIOR ELEVATIONS shown in the four drawings (below) represent the bedroom situation in the floor plan.

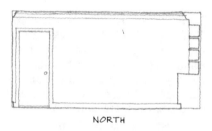

NORTH

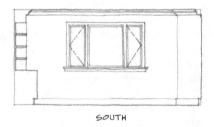

SOUTH

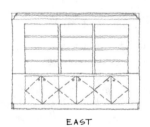

EAST

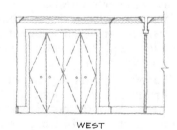

WEST

ADDITIONAL CLEARANCE

3'-0"

2'-0"

3'-0"

MINIMUM CLEARANCES between pieces of bedroom furniture serve as guidelines for room arrangement.

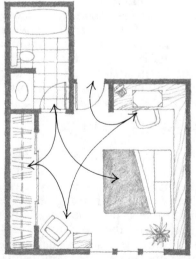

TRAFFIC PATTERNS within the bedroom should be planned to save you time and motion.

Small Bedrooms & Guest Rooms

For a guest or for yourself,
tuck a bed into a tight corner

Your brother and sister-in-law and their two children are taking you up on your invitation—their vacation will be at your house. You have an extra bedroom, but it's the size of a closet. What can you do to make them comfortable?

Guest rooms and small bedrooms have a number of elements in common. In either, you'll probably want a space-saving bed and other furnishings that make the best use of the square footage available. Most of the information presented here deals with closet-sized bedrooms, but you'll find ideas for giving visiting relatives a comfortable place to sleep.

About guest rooms

A true guest room—a separate bedroom especially set up for the care and comfort of house guests—is a thing of the past for most of us. These days, if a house is big enough to provide an extra bedroom, the room isn't used only to accommodate guests. It's also a place to watch television, study, or sew. The aunt from out of state and old friends from college have to fit in where they can.

The longer guests stay, the more important privacy becomes, both for them and for the homeowners. If the guest room is a multipur-

pose room, its other uses shouldn't be pressing. For example, you might plan on moving the sewing machine or putting the television somewhere else when guests arrive. Good soundproofing makes for a better guest room. Also, a thermostat independent of the house's heating system—or a separate heat-efficient fireplace or wood stove—adds guest-pleasing custom comfort.

Guests would love to have their own bathroom and sitting room, of course. But on a smaller scale, you can provide many things easily and inexpensively to make them comfortable: a bedside clock, current magazines, tissues, a bowl of fruit, fresh flowers. Touches of luxury could include a small refrigerator suitably stocked or a coffee pot set up to plug in and perk in the morning.

Furnishing to fit

Probably the best remedy for a too-small bedroom is to build in the furnishings, especially if you don't expect your storage needs or the room's purpose to change much over the next few years. Some built-in features such as adjustable shelves or a multipurpose counter (dressing table, work surface, desk) offer more flexibil-

ity, and wall systems that only look built-in are great for less permanent situations. To keep a built-in unit from looking too massive (and making the room seem oppressive) alternate its open and closed compartments.

SHELVES FROM FLOOR TO CEILING *organize necessities; here shelves also act as a see-through divider.*

A very different solution to cramped quarters is to pare down the bedroom furnishings to as few as possible. You could, as the Japanese do, leave the bedroom essentially bare of furnishings, bringing them in only when they are actually used (see photographs on page 21).

Another approach is to get rid of clutter. Enclosing storage and minimizing pictures, plants, objects, and accessories bring relief to an overcrowded room. Also, illusion—mirrors and colors that are light or reflective—can make a small space seem bigger. Coordinated fabrics, colors, and furniture design will pull a room together, too.

Consider fitting separate pieces of furniture with casters. A dresser blocking a seldom-used closet, for example, could be moved out of the way quickly when necessary.

Doors can be another factor in space-efficiency. The best ones for a small bedroom are sliding, folding, and pocket doors—or you can use curtains or shades as doors. You can also free space inside the room by rehanging a door to swing outward or by removing it entirely. A door located near a corner will interfere with furniture less than one in the middle of a wall. Adding a hinge-stop to a door will allow you to place furniture behind it (see drawing).

If you want a bed with a headboard or footboard, consider using the reverse side of it as a van-ity, bookshelf, or room divider. (You'll find more information on beds on the next three pages.)

Bedside tables take up less room if they're attached to the bed or mounted on the wall. The project on page 55 shows bedside tables that stack up high; the tables to build on page 31 attach to a headboard or a wall.

An efficient small bedroom has a comfortable sleeping space, adequate storage with easy access, and enough floor space in which to comfortably dress and move around. The drawing on page 13 gives you standard clearances between typical separate pieces of bedroom furniture. This chapter shows you ways to take up even less space.

Properly planned and outfitted, your "too-small" bedroom may even surprise you: it might actually be free of wasted floor space, economical to heat, and

DRESSER ROLLS away from in front of a seldom-used closet; bed and other furniture move easily on casters.

FOOT-OF-THE-BED FURNITURE gives a finished look to the bed and adds extra storage in a small room.

REFLECTIONS from a mirrored head-of-the-bed wall, plus clutter-free surfaces make this room appear larger.

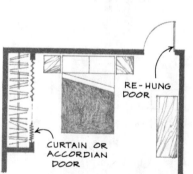

RE-HUNG DOOR

CURTAIN OR ACCORDIAN DOOR

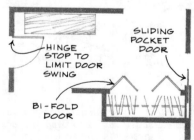

HINGE STOP TO LIMIT DOOR SWING

SLIDING POCKET DOOR

BI-FOLD DOOR

RETHINK THE DOORS into the bedroom or on closets; you may discover ways to free some extra inches.

AS AN ALTERNATIVE to a bedside table, these wall-hugging shelves hold lots, free floor space.

easy to maintain. We may eventually find that bigger is not necessarily better, and the huge bedroom could go the way of the block-long sedan.

Space-saving beds

Fold them, inflate them, pivot them, roll them away, stack them, convert them—beds don't have to take up valuable floor space when they're not being slept on.

Most of us think of a sofa bed first when we need a space-conserving sleep spot, but there are many other quite comfortable possibilities.

If you prefer a standard bed, it can still take up less space visually. A low bed or one without a headboard, footboard, posts, or canopy will appear relatively small.

Guest beds and small-space beds differ in the amount of use they receive. A continually used small-space bed will require a better-wearing mattress than an occasionally used guest bed. And be sure a small-space bed used every night is easy to set up.

Sofa, chair & love seat fold-out beds

We're most familiar with sofa beds that conceal a standard mattress. But love seats and chairs that turn into beds are also available; often they're constructed of foam cushions instead of springs. For more information about spring mattresses, see pages 10–11; the advantages and disadvantages of foam are discussed on page 10.

Furniture-beds with springs are of two types. One uses a jackknife-principle mechanism, where the back drops down level with the seat to form a bed. With the other type, the convertible, the bed fits inside a couch and must be pulled out. The jackknife design is smaller and less expensive, but the convertible type is generally more comfortable.

Foam cushion furniture-beds in their simplest form are stacked or rolled-up foam slabs. They may be linked to each other with fabric on the principle of the Japanese *shiki-buton* (see drawing below). Other foam beds are simply folded up and strapped into place to make a chair or couch.

Foam cushion furniture-beds are within the scope of many home sewers (see the *Sunset* book *How to Make Pillows* for directions).

Before you buy any kind of furniture-bed, test it to see if it's easy to make into a bed.

Air beds

There are a few styles of these on the market, though they're not widely available—you'll find them primarily through mail-order advertising in magazines and at water bed stores. They come in several sizes, and operate like the air mattresses used in swimming pools: you inflate them with air to use them (a bicycle pump is useful), and deflate them to store. When folded, they take up very little space.

Some have a fabriclike finish over the plastic airbag.

Beds built in layers: Bunkbeds & trundle beds

As beds reserved for guests, bunkbeds and trundle beds save space during the day, yet give a restful night's sleep. Either is also

PAIRED CHAIRS give no hint that they convert into twin beds, supplying extra spots for sleeping.

FLIP AND FOLD—foam cushions change from attractive seating to sleeping space; just add sheets and blankets.

WHEN IT'S INFLATED, an air bed requires no special frame. Just fold it up to store during the day.

LAYERED BUNKBEDS are a space-saving favorite for children's rooms; agile adults could use them as well.

NOW YOU SEE THEM, now you don't. These low beds disappear under a platform, roll out when needed.

a workable every-night bed, if you're gymnastically inclined.

Bunkbeds are typically used in children's bedrooms, but adults can certainly take advantage of their clever concept as well. The top-bunk occupant must climb a ladder to get into bed. Depending on the bed's design, the user of the lower bunk may have to be careful not to bump his head as he climbs into bed.

Trundle beds wheel out from underneath another bed. Out of necessity, they're close to the ground. The mattress on a trundle bed (or bunkbed) stays flat, so it remains comfortable longer than one that must be folded and compressed.

The Murphy bed idea

Patented in 1905, the original Murphy bed was such a popular success that its name has become a generic term. The Murphy bed pivoted up into a closet, was reasonably easy to operate, and freed floor space for daytime use.

Manufacturers today make beds that tilt into bookcases and various styles of cabinets. Some beds are hinged at the head, others at the side.

A bed that disappears behind attractive cabinetry is pictured on page 20.

Another kind of bed that spends most of its time out of sight is the fold-away bed. It takes up little space when stored and is easily wheeled out for overnight guests. (You can also find fold-aways at rental outlets.) Since the mattress is actually folded, it will wear out faster than one that stays flat.

MODERN MURPHY BED emerges from a wall; other part-time beds vanish into bookcases or cabinets at dawn.

Window seats (built-in beds) & day beds

Instead of disappearing, these beds metamorphose into daytime furniture. Certain compromises in design and comfort are needed to make them serve both purposes— window seats are likely to be a bit narrow for a bed and day beds a bit too deep for a sitting spot. (Of course, you can add pillows and cushions as backrests.)

(Continued on next page)

WHETHER YOU RENT one when guests are due or keep your own for frequent use, a fold-away bed offers convenience.

DEEP WINDOW SEAT changes into a bed at night. By day, a pile of pillows makes it a pleasant place to sit.

Some of these beds can be left made up, with a covering that's removed at night.

Two twin beds arranged in an L-shape make a flexible day bed arrangement for a guest room. Turn the mattress of a day bed often so one edge doesn't wear out faster than the other.

TWIN BEDS for twin uses—these studio couches tuck under a corner table, pull out for use as extra beds.

GO NATIVE with a hammock to swing and sway you to sleep. For a sunny snooze, put another on deck or patio.

LOFTY BEDROOM RETREAT has additional privacy when shades or blinds are hung from rafters.

Hammocks & hanging beds

Using vertical space instead of floor space, these sleeping spots take some getting used to for most of us—we're apprehensive about rolling over in them and ending up on the floor.

Big hammocks, designed for a night's sleep rather than an afternoon nap, might be the answer. Almost any sturdy, washable fabric—even woven yarn or rope—could be used to make a hammock. Just be sure the ends are attached to a strong section of house structure. Hammocks are exotic and decorative, yet relatively easy to handle—light enough to move out of the way in the morning.

Hanging beds needn't be precarious either. Unlike hammocks, they can have a solid base. Using a pulley system, you can rig one up so it's high against the ceiling during the day, allowing room to walk underneath it. For safety, lower it almost to the floor when you want to sleep on it.

HANGING BED, securely fastened, can be raised or lowered as needed. Room gains added floor space.

Loft bedrooms

A building trend that makes sense in small living quarters is the loft bedroom. Like a balcony, a loft overlooks living space below. You reach it by climbing up a ladder or a stairway.

Lofts are especially useful as an addition to a high-ceilinged house. Plenty of headroom underneath the bedroom loft and between it and the ceiling makes the arrangement most comfortable. You can use a bed loft with less vertical height, but you may bump your head climbing into it. If space is really tight, perhaps you should leave the loft to your children. Consider, too, that your local building code may have some headroom specifications.

Privacy is an important concern if you're planning a loft bedroom. Lofts seem to work best in one or two-person houses; if your family is larger, you'll need to plan shutters over interior windows or find other ways to close off light and noise from the rest of the house.

Photographs showing loft bedrooms are on pages 22 and 30.

Topping a bank of drawers and cabinets with a foam mattress creates a minimum-space bed. Desk extension incorporates steps used to climb up to the bed. Windows—located wherever possible—and skylights make this built-into-a-hillside bedroom a bright, enjoyable place to be. Architect: Violeta Autumn.

Built-in beds free space in small bedrooms

You'd never guess that this used to be a utility porch. Since acquiring guest quarters was more of a priority for the owners than having a utility sink, they built a bed right over it. Fabric skirting the bed pulls aside to reveal storage space.

Cramped? Not at all: built-in look of bed, a skylight, and side windows all contribute to unenclosed effect. Architect: Kirby Ward Fitzpatrick.

Etched mirrors inset into custom oak cabinet doors gleam reflections back into cottage.
As shown here, floor space is available during the day for furniture or simply
for moving about without having a bed in the way.

Now you see them, now you don't—
beds disappear during the day

Doors folded back, cabinet reveals a tilt-up bed. Most beds of this type are light and easy to maneuver. Some can be left with bedding in place when they're inside cabinet.

Completely set up, bed takes the place of the rocking chair in the first picture. Niche built into side of cabinet contains a lamp. Designer: Jerry Cebe.

During the day, panels slide open to merge the rooms and bring in sunshine. Bed (below) has been folded and stored, replaced by table set for tea. Lightweight furniture is moved in when needed and removed when not in use, allowing one room to serve many different functions. Glass windows are used extensively. Architects: Sohn-Nakahira. Interior designer: Bruce Nakahira.

Traditional Japanese bed of thick quilts *(futons)* over folding cushions *(shiki-buton)* occupies room shown above during sleeping hours. Sliding, grass-cloth-covered panels and shoji screens create a room within a room, an enclosed sleeping space. Room design uses 3 by 6-foot basic dimension and features Douglas fir exposed beams and peeled pine poles, traditional *tatami* mats and *tokonama* (art display alcove).

Lofts are for sleeping

Right now it's a skylight seat. Later in the day it can be a bed. By building in the upstairs seat, owners were able to fit in shelves on two sides and utilize a stair landing. Architect: Charles Vos.

Openings—to the living room below, to the stairwell, to a skylight—characterize this sleeping loft. Barrier below handrail is a series of cables strung between hooks. Kilim-pattern rug makes a decorative headboard. Architect: Peter W. Behn.

Fresh as spring—painting on the wall, vase of freesias, and strawberry print sheets bring color to serenely white sleeping loft. Ledge on two sides of bed forms convenient surface to hold flowers and books. Designer: John I. Matthias.

Headboard cabinet has a slanting backrest

You can lean back at a comfortable angle against the slanting front of this headboard cabinet. To make it even more restful, fasten pillows to the backrest with strips of nylon self-gripping fastener. The backrest opens to expose a storage shelf within the headboard. This shelf hinges so that you can store large items like pillows underneath it (small things would be difficult to reach).

On page 31 are directions for two side tables with slanting fronts. Attach the side tables to this headboard cabinet and you'll have a great-looking head-of-the-bed assemblage.

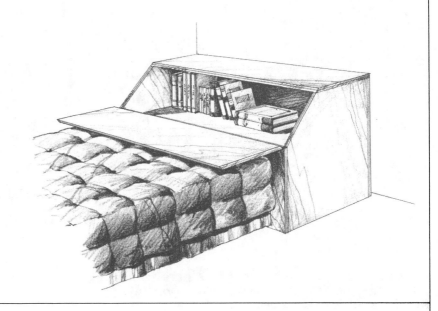

To make this headboard, first cut the two side panels (A) from ¾" plywood. (Before cutting all pieces, make sure best side of plywood will be exposed.) Each panel is 24" wide. To establish their height measurement, add 12" to the height of your bed from the floor. As shown, cut off one corner of each side piece at 45°. From ¾" plywood, cut the front (B), the top (C), and the back (D) to a length 2" more than the width of your bed. Cut these three pieces to the widths that will fit accurately on the edges of (A) where they belong. Bevel the leading edge of (C) at 45°.

Subtract 1½" from the length measurement of (B) to arrive at the proper length for the bottom (E). This piece should be 24" wide, the same as the (A) pieces. Cut it from ¾" plywood. Glue and nail these sections (A, B, C, D, and E) together, using 6d finishing nails.

From the plywood, cut the door (F) to the same length as (C) and (B) but make the long edge cuts at 45° angles so that (F) will fit correctly over the top edge of (B) and

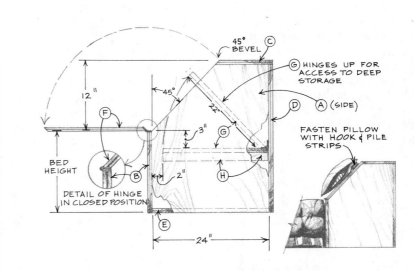

in front of the leading edge of (C).

Cut the ¾" plywood shelf (G) 22" wide and ¼" shorter than the length of the bottom (E). Also cut two 22"-long cleats (H) from 1 by 3 stock for holding the shelf 3" below the level of the opening. Glue and nail the cleats in place onto (A). Using a continuous hinge, fasten the shelf (G) to the back (D) as detailed. Hinge the

front door in place with a continuous hinge as shown.

Set all nail heads. Fill edges and nail holes, and sand where required. Paint with enamel. Add a cabinet pull high on the door.

If you wish, fasten small strips of nylon self-gripping fastener to the face of the door and put their mates on pillow cases. This way, you can secure pillows to the slanted surface.

Bedroom Offices & Sewing Places

In the bedroom's peace and quiet,
stitch a seam or review a report

If you need an undisturbed spot to concentrate on correspondence, finish your child's Halloween costume, or tackle your bank balance, why not plan a workplace in the bedroom? With square footage becoming more and more expensive, using the bedroom for more than one purpose makes sense. And because bedrooms are more private than other rooms, you'll have fewer interruptions and you can leave your work in process.

Where to put the workplace

Your work area can be a room next to the bedroom, a space shared with the sleeping quarters, or even a structure combined with the bed.

A study or studio next to the bedroom, separated by a door, has double virtue—association with a bedroom's privacy, plus all the advantages of a separate room.

Putting your work spot around a corner from the bed or just having it face away from the bed will separate the two zones. A change in floor level will also serve that purpose.

An extra closet—an already-built-in alcove—is a natural spot to convert to a tiny bedroom office. Using it won't rob the bedroom of floor space, though it may create a shortage of clothes storage space. Depending on its type, you may need to alter the existing door to give you use of the whole closet.

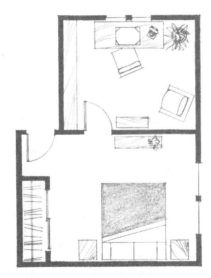

A GOOD PLACE TO CONCENTRATE, separate room adjacent to the bedroom makes an ideal workplace.

FACING AWAY from the rest of the bedroom, built-in counter is a desk now, adaptable for other purposes later.

CLOSETED where clothes used to be, hideaway work spot can disappear behind folding doors.

Some people like to work on, or even in, the bed. If you're one of them, make it convenient by installing bedside work surfaces, communications such as a telephone and intercom, and effective lighting. You'll need a durable, cleanable bedspread, too. Bed-desk combinations include a two-level bed island with a bunk above and a work surface below, or work surfaces surrounding the bed (see photograph on page 29).

Of course, a bedroom workplace can be simply a desk or table anywhere in the room. The following sections can help you decide exactly where to put it and how to set it up.

FOR THE ULTIMATE in space-saving, consider this idea for layering a desk and a place to sleep.

Reconciling work with sleep

There are two drawbacks to setting up a workplace in the bedroom: the clutter greeting you first thing each morning, and, in a shared bedroom, the other person's need for repose.

NOW YOU SEE a desk ready for work; with the hinged panel closed, the desk disappears.

To eliminate the visual blight, you can close it away, cover it up, or screen it: Consider a desk with a roll top, drop front, or some other form of closure. Use a decorative typewriter cover (keeps dust off, too). Store supplies in drawers or cupboards that you close when you take a break. Or use attractive storage such as ethnic baskets or bright plastic containers.

A partition of some kind will make your bedroom appear smaller but tidier. A partial wall or storage island decorated in keeping with the rest of the room will contain work debris. A fabric panel suspended from the ceiling makes a thin, light partition; you could use a shade or blind to pull down when necessary. Roller shades can have a "finished" look both front and back; Austrian, Roman, and balloon shades, though decorative, are less attractive from the back. Portable screens fold out of the way when you want to open up the work area, and they hide your ongoing project when you want to forget about it.

If the whir of the sewing machine or plink of the calculator will disturb someone else's sleep, try setting up some kind of sound barrier. Soft surfaces such as fabric, carpeting, and rugs will help absorb noise; so will irregular

NO CARPENTRY SKILLS were needed to bring in this desk; next to a window, it shares natural light with the bed.

USE GOOD-LOOKING BASKETS or other containers you like for storing work supplies attractively.

CABINET SEPARATES bed from desk in a room large enough to subdivide into two distinct areas.

surfaces such as bookshelves. Hard, smooth surfaces, on the other hand, accentuate noise. If you have a visual barrier, you may be able to use it as a sound barrier also.

ROLLER SHADE room divider (it could be Roman, Austrian, or balloon style) hangs from the ceiling.

Illuminating your work

Assuming you have overall bedroom lighting already planned (see pages 56–62), now is the time to consider task lighting. You want to direct light onto your telephone book, needle and thread, or paint brush without shining it into your eyes, either directly or by reflection.

Natural light from the north gives the most even, glare-free illumination. Bounced natural light from other points of the compass is second best. On pages 48–54 you'll find information on using windows and skylights to bring in natural light.

For working at night or in situations where you can't use natural light, plan the artificial lighting carefully. Best way to avoid shining light right into your eyes is to put the light source behind you. If you sit at an L-shaped or U-shaped desk, the fixture should be adjustable. To eliminate shadows, direct light over your left shoulder if you're right-handed, over your right shoulder if you're left-handed.

To prevent reflected glare, keep your light source a good distance from your work. Shielding the light source with a diffuser such as a fabric shade will also cut down glare.

In a shared bedroom, plan to keep the pool of light around your desk from overflowing onto the other person's closed eyes.

Setting up the workplace

A bedroom workplace, just like one elsewhere, calls for efficient storage and a well-thought-out work flow arrangement. Spend some time thinking about your work flow; a clear idea of the sequence in which you use your equipment and materials will help you decide where to put your storage and your work surface. You should be able to reach everything you need while sitting at your work spot—the more frequently something is used, the easier it should be to get to.

Built-in storage—or as close to built-in storage as you can get—is particularly space-efficient.

BUILT-IN BOOKSHELF, tall closet next to it, and under-counter cupboards keep work supplies within easy reach.

Experiment with the height of the work surface to find what's comfortable for you. A chair that supports your lower back is a wise choice.

If your work area is a continuation of the rest of the room design, it will be less obtrusive. Complementary fabrics and finishes will blend it with the sleeping part of the room.

PORTABLE SCREEN can be toted around the room, opened out or folded away to change bedroom configuration.

SHEDDING SOME LIGHT on the subject, adjustable desk lamp illumines at the best angle for the task.

Select a fabric or apply an appliqué in an added-on alcove that inspires creativity. Wallpaper dresses up sewing area, blends it with rest of bedroom—even the storage boxes are covered in small-print paper. Track lights and floor lamp behind woman supplement window light at the work center. Design: Reo Haynes.

Annex a workplace to your bedroom, in an alcove or along a wall

Step up to the bed from the desk in a small adjacent room. Office is lower than bedroom so view through office window (not shown) can be seen from the bed. Louvered doors at right conceal closet space. Architect: Donald King Loomis.

Gaily wrapped presents and sewing projects take shape at this built-in work counter and storage wall. Drawer at left is extra-wide to hold rolls of wrapping paper; open drawer below machine contains spools of thread on upright dowels. Sewing instructions are pinned to fabric-covered fiberboard. Architects: Fisher-Friedman Associates. Interior designer: Randee Seiger.

Desks for two wait behind the shelving partition. He "likes to work in a cave," so his desk faces the wall; she likes to look outside, so her desk has a window looking into the garden.

Divide one room into sleep zone and work sphere

In sleeping area, fresh green of bed, bedspread, and chest brightens white-painted room. Shelf sections act as a partition; there are more cubicles on desk side. Open ceiling beams add overhead interest, give spacious effect. This bedroom addition reused a maple floor from a school. Architect: Harry Rodda of Spencer/Lee/Busse.

Around-the-bed studio is built of 14 bolted-together birch plywood modules. Compressing bed, office, and storage into one piece of furniture left a walkway around the unit and easy access to supplies in the small (12 by 13-foot) room (see below left).

Thoughtful furniture arrangement yields office space

Flat files pull out from underneath the bed shown above. Partially enclosed by backs of desks, the bed has a tilting headboard, extended platform, and cubbyhole for radio. Architect: Jennifer Clements of Robert Herman Associates.

Floor-to-ceiling books backdrop the desk in this combination bedroom and office. The furniture separates parts of the room: a comfortable couch backs up to the businesslike desk. Ceiling was removed to extend bedroom upward into the attic. Architect: George Cody. Interior designer: Stewart Morton.

Handsome sliding doors divide bedroom and office, while rich-hued carpet connects the rooms. The old oak doors are fitted with owner-made leaded glass. Use of wood on both wall and ceiling at entrance adds drama.
Architect: William B. Remick.

Step into the office in the next room

Up a level, loft studio shares sunlight with the bedroom below, thanks to a skylight over the loft (behind canvas shade). Ladder with red handrail leads up to studio. Overhang above the bed is finished with rough-sawn boards.
Architect: Robert J. Geering.

Across a skylighted stairwell from each other are wood-trimmed sewing room and bedroom, with bathroom beyond. Interior windows which let you look from bedroom to sewing room are fitted with curtains.
Architect: William B. Remick.

Slanting side tables to add to your bed

You can use these versatile side tables two different ways. Attached to the wall or to a flat headboard, they line up right next to your pillows. Used in combination with the slanting headboard described on page 47, they sit behind the bed. Their design complements the headboard: slanting surfaces align parallel to each other. The side tables provide ample surface area for a cup of coffee or a book when open, and look trim and attractive when closed.

Make the side tables from high-quality ¾" plywood, cut with the best side outward.

Cut four 10½" by 24" rectangles for the side pieces (A). Cut off end of one side piece at a 45° angle from one corner. Use this piece as a pattern for marking and cutting the other three side pieces.

Cut two 11¼" by 24" rectangles for the back pieces (B). Cut two top (C) and two bottom pieces (D), measuring the exact distances where they will fit along the edges of (A). Be sure to allow an extra ¾" for the top where it will overlap the back; also add an extra ¾" to the bottom for the bevel on the front. Bevel the front edges of (C) and (D) at a 45° angle, as shown.

Assemble top, bottom, and sides of each side table as shown in the drawing, using glue and 6d finishing nails. Wipe off any excess glue. Measure for, and cut, the doors (E). In the drawing, you'll see that both top and bottom edges of (E) are beveled at 45°.

Set all nail heads. Fill nail holes and plywood edges; sand the edges. Paint with enamel.

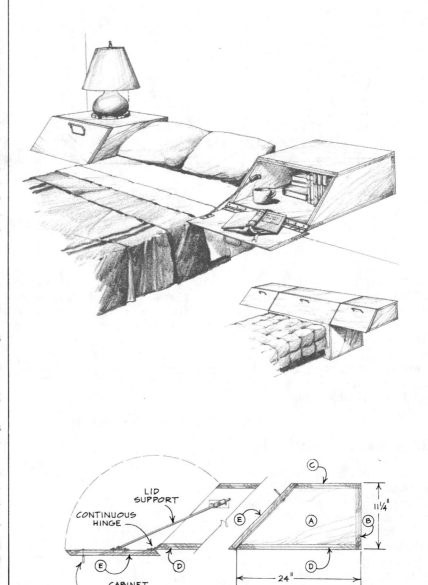

Hinge the doors to the cabinets as shown. Add folding lid supports for locking the doors in a level, open position. Attach a cabinet pull to the face of each door.

Mount the finished side tables to the headboard, using bolts, washers, and nuts, or attach them to the wall, using lag screws and washers.

Bedroom Sitting Areas

*For a place to chat, take tea,
or just doze by the fire*

Just moving a comfortable chair into the bedroom turns the room into a sitting area as well as a sleeping space. As a place to light while putting on your shoes, a spot for a friend to settle and chat, or just as a handy surface to lay out tomorrow's outfit, a sitting area is a valuable addition to a bedroom.

How separate should it be?

A sitting room that's right *off* the bedroom rather than right *in* it has several advantages. You can close the door between the two rooms, reserving the bed chamber itself just for sleeping. With a wide doorway between the two rooms, the sitting room can be an extension of the bedroom, to close off or connect as you wish. A sliding or folding door between the two rooms can serve well. In a large bedroom, the sitting room could be behind a movable screen or partition.

But there are also advantages to having the sitting area completely open to the bed portion of the room. For instance, you won't have to worry about the visual effect or the lighting problems that

can accompany a chopped-up space. And the main purpose of the sitting area might be to allow interaction through the whole room. In a small bedroom especially, a sitting room that's really part of the bedroom is a wise use of space.

Planning the seating

To do the basic job—add sitting space to the bedroom—many

ALTER AN ALCOVE and gain seating. Just add flush overhead lights, wall lamp, comfortable furniture.

people simply pop a chaise longue into a corner. This piece of furniture is a favorite for bedrooms, its luxurious lines especially appropriate for drowsing off. In the same way, a comfortable chair with an ottoman or footstool lets you put your feet up.

Portable lighting is what you need if you use separate pieces of furniture in your sitting area. Floor lamps are as easy to fit into a bedroom as a single chair. Run

DOORS DIVIDE sitting and sleeping space. When the doors are opened, two rooms seem to work together as one.

the cord along the wall until it reaches an outlet.

A table accompanying the chair makes a surface on which to rest a book and a table lamp. A table or two can also be a cozy place to serve a continental breakfast or a late-night snack.

Built-in seating economizes on space, and a simple way to achieve that seating is to vary the floor levels—especially effective in combination with a platform bed. Any number of level variations are possible, from a single extra level to three or four levels of different widths and heights. Carpeting and rugs are most comfortable to sit on, but cool tile or wood supplemented with pillows can serve your purpose.

More traditional built-in seating arrangements are banquettes along walls, or window seats. Though you can't rearrange such seating, it can be better integrated into the rest of the room than movable chairs and sofas.

If you're planning to install a fireplace, an especially good case can be made for built-in seating. Obviously you're not going to be moving the fireplace around. Once you establish the best place for the seating in relation to the fireplace, it may as well be permanent.

With built-in seating, using ceiling or wall light fixtures will avoid unsightly cords.

STEP DOWN to a sitting area. A conversation pit built into a large bedroom makes the bed-sitting room.

Focus on a fireplace or wood stove

Flickering firelight followed by the glow of ebbing coals can lull anyone to sleep. And what could be cozier than a cheery blaze on a wintry morning?

A fireplace or wood stove in the bedroom contributes special warmth, both actual and esthetic. Bedroom fireplaces fall into two categories: those that are the focal point of a bedroom sitting area, and those that are to be viewed from the bed. A raised fireplace is easier to watch from a bed, and it can also be an element of the sitting area if the change in height doesn't bother you. Whatever height the fireplace opening is, a flush hearth (level with the floor) will save floor space in a small bedroom.

Fire-view wood stoves let you enjoy watching the fire while it warms. Some of these have glass fronts; with others, metal doors swing open.

With a fireplace or stove come the problems of wood supply and storage and of ash removal. A fleecy white bedroom rug won't last long in the same room as a heavily used fireplace unless you have a way to bring wood in and take ashes out without tramping over the rug. If your fireplace is on an outside wall, you might install a wood storage bin with access from both inside and outside the house. With an ash pit, ashes can be removed from the outside. Also, if your bedroom is upstairs, seriously consider installing a dumbwaiter instead of lugging logs up the stairs. (See the *Sunset* books *Homeowner's Guide to Wood Stoves* and *How to Plan & Build Fireplaces*.)

The options in ways to bring a fire into the bedroom are, in terms of the way they heat: 1) a conventional built-in fireplace, prefabricated or constructed of masonry; 2) a heat-circulating fireplace (many styles available); 3) a freestanding fireplace; and 4) a wood stove. See the photographs on pages 35, 37, 38, 43.

Adding a fireplace

Installing a fireplace in the bedroom may be easier than you think, especially if you use a prefabricated one (conventional built-in fireplaces are much more complex to add). A prefabricated fire-

BED'S-EYE VIEW of flickering flames is best when there's a raised hearth or the fireplace is inset high in a wall.

FREESTANDING FIREPLACE not only brings cheer to a bedroom sitting area, but also can heat the room in winter.

place doesn't weigh much (perhaps 600 to 800 pounds, depending on its decorative facing); in many cases, it can be installed on an inside wall or on a second floor without the need to reinforce the house structure. Prefabricated fireplaces come in both freestanding and built-in models, with or without integral heat circulators. Most built-in prefabricated fireplaces allow zero clearance between the firebox and combustible house walls, and can be faced with almost any material. They need no additional insulation.

The freestanding type of prefabricated fireplace is generally less expensive to buy and easier to install than a built-in one because the house will have to be opened up in only one place—for the chimney. Seating can encircle a freestanding fireplace that is attractively finished on all sides.

Using a fireplace or wood stove for heating

If you're serious about warming the bedroom with wood heat, you should know that with a conventional fireplace close to 90 percent of the fire's heat is lost up the chimney. Of the three ways to achieve efficient wood heat, the best is a wood stove; you could also install a prefabricated heat-circulating fireplace, or add one or more heat-recovery devices to an existing fireplace. With any of these three choices, the bedroom will cool down after the fire dies out (an untended fire will generate heat for at least an hour, sometimes up to 12 hours). You could add a warm down comforter or wool blankets to the bed and relight the fire in the morning, or use the main heating system to warm the bedroom through the night.

Be sure to size the fireplace or stove to the bedroom. Many heat circulators, for example, put out much more warmth than necessary for a 10 by 12-foot bedroom. Of course, surplus heat can be vented to adjoining rooms. A fireplace dealer can suggest the best size for your situation.

Wood-burning stoves range from charming antique parlor stoves to very utilitarian-looking devices. Fire-view stoves let you see the flames through glass or past opened metal doors. You can use some wood stoves to heat a pan or a teapot—handy for preparing a hot drink late at night or first thing in the morning.

For help in choosing the best size, style, and placement of a stove to heat the bedroom, use the *Sunset* book *Homeowner's Guide to Wood Stoves* and give a stove dealer accurate information about the bedroom: a precise floor plan showing room shape and size, including ceiling height; location, size, and shape of windows and doors; which walls are exterior and which interior; thickness, type, and location of insulation; and probable furniture arrangement in the bedroom.

A stove's placement—like that of a fireplace—will be limited to where you can run the flue pipe and install the chimney. Stove and hearth will be an integral part of the bedroom design, so placement should be convenient and attractive.

Heat-circulating fireplaces are available as variations of many prefabricated fireplace designs. Guaranteed not to smoke, they draw in cool air from indoors or outside through inlets, then distribute heated air through vents. The air ducts of some heat-circulating fireplaces can be extended to distribute warmth to other rooms.

Heat-recovery devices that you can add easily to an existing bedroom fireplace include optimum radiation grates, tempered glass screens, convection grates, and metal heat reflectors. Units are available that combine these devices, such as a glass screen with convection grate and attached circulating fan. Or you can buy devices separately and combine them yourself.

PUT THE KETTLE on your wood stove and soon you'll have tea for two—as well as toasty toes—without leaving the room.

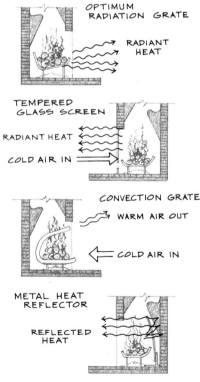

ADDING A HEAT-RECOVERY DEVICE to your bedroom fireplace increases heating efficiency, cuts costs.

Story-telling corner consists of pair of blue upholstered armchairs, matching
ottoman, and reading light from a table lamp. This is a solar house: warmth travels up from below
through the stairwell and the spaces left between floor and walls. Heat-circulating fireplace
supplements the sun's energy. Architect: Burr E. Nash.

Within-the-bedroom seating centers on the fireplace

Just enough: a lamp, a place to sit, and a no-hearth
fireplace to sit beside. Green bedspread and chair fabric
add verdant notes to cool white bedroom. Trestle beam
incorporates overhead lighting.
Architect: William W. Hedley, Jr.

Relaxed brunch-munchers take advantage of lounging spot created by
flow of carpeting over steps. Serene bedroom has cream-colored ceramic
tile around fireplace. Pale beige suede-like fabric covers custom bed and
side table; clear acrylic sheet protects tabletop. At right, chromed
column shines light back into room—bulbs are set behind downward
ceiling extension. Architect: Glenn B. Pollock.

Not quite two rooms, not really one; bedroom and sitting room are combined

Looking from sitting room into the bedroom, you see handsome built-in cabinetry of Honduras mahogany. In remodeling, wall between the two rooms (see below) was opened up.

View back toward sitting room shows bookcase wall and door to living room overlook. Remodeling kept intact the integrity of house originally designed by Bernard Maybeck.
Architect: Thaddeus E. Kusmierski.

Sipping morning coffee and sharing conversation take place in living area removed from bedroom by
partial wall that contains a chimney for the wood stove, a bookcase, and closets on the bedroom side.
Living area is a guest room, too—the day bed was designed by the owner.
Architect: Gordon Drake. Design: Maggie Baylis.

Here's a place where the owner can read, watch television, or listen to music in comfort.
Added onto a small bedroom, sitting area extends just 9 feet out.
Designer: Richard Pennington.

Hidden beneath the window seat is storage compartment for pillows or extra bedding. With wall light, seat is comfortable spot for reading, writing. Architect: William J. Zimmerman.

Simple bench with cushion and pillows lends itself to fireside contemplation; window seat upholstery matches bedspread fabric. Wood trim accents the windows; flower-painted tile adds charm to fireplace. Architects: Fisher-Friedman Associates. Interior designer: Randee Seiger.

Window seats belong in bedrooms

Turning a corner, windows and skylights follow line of L-shaped window seat. Movable seat and back cushions make this a comfortable place to curl up. Light and views through the glass animate the corner. Architect: Robert J. Geering. Interior designer: Sandra York.

Triangular headboard fits into a corner

Tired of the same old furniture arrangement? Turning your bed on the diagonal will add some novelty to your night life. Fill the corner behind the head of the bed with this headboard-shelf structure. (More corner headboard ideas are pictured on pages 61 and 68.)

An easy way to finish this headboard is to paint it a color that complements the rest of your bedroom decorating. Another alternative is to use wallpaper or fabric: Cover the headboard with the same paper or fabric used on the bedroom walls, and it will blend into the background. Or use a contrasting paper or fabric to make it stand out.

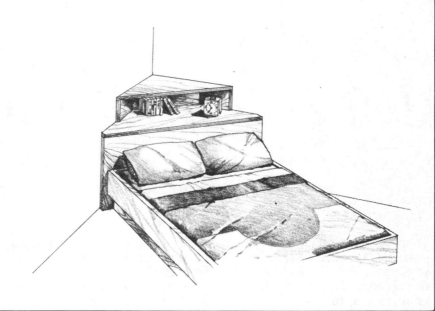

This corner cabinet-headboard is designed for a 72-inch-wide king-size bed. If your bed is smaller or larger, be sure to change the plans accordingly: length across the front should be 2" more than your bed's width; height to the first shelf should be 12" more than your bed's mattress height from the floor.

Build the cabinet from ¾" plywood. (Be sure to face the best side of all pieces outward.) First, cut the front (A)—it is a simple rectangle, 74" long and 12" higher than the top of your mattress. Next, cut the sides (B) so they will butt join at a 90° angle at the back (one is ¾" longer than the other to allow proper overlap). The sides are 10¼" higher than the front (A). Make 45° cuts along the front edges of (B) for joining them to (A).

Cut the shelf (C) as illustrated. Use it as a guide for marking the length of the corner cutouts in (B). Cut out those corners; the front edge of the cutouts must be cut at 45°. Glue and nail together the sides (B) to front (A), using 8d

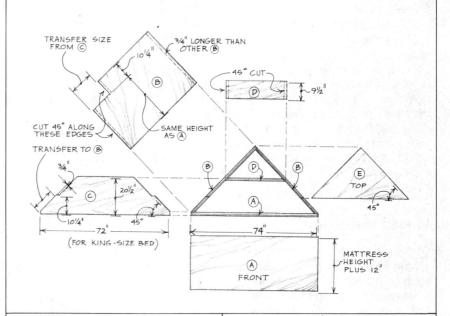

finishing nails. Then glue and nail (C) where it belongs.

Measure for the proper length of the shelf back (D) and cut it. Remember to make the end cuts at 45°. Set (D) in place on (C) to be sure its top edge sits flush with the top edges of (B). Glue and nail (C) to (D) and (B) to (D).

Set a piece of plywood on top and mark it for fit (E). Cut (E), then glue and nail it to the top edges of (B) and (D).

Set all nail heads below the surface and fill with wood putty. Sand and fill where necessary, especially along the exposed plywood edges. Paint with enamel.

Bed & Bath Combinations

*For sounder sleeping and better bathing,
ally the house's two private rooms*

There's something wonderfully sybaritic about a designed-as-a-whole bedroom and bathroom combination. Fortunately, it's an arrangement that is also eminently practical and one that doesn't require a suite of spectacular proportions.

It can be done in a number of ways. One bathroom can be shared by two or more bedrooms, with compartmented fixtures adding flexibility. The completely private bathroom adjoining the bedroom has long been the ideal. Another alternative is a bathroom fixture or two—such as an extra sink or a special tub—right in the bedroom.

Shared bathrooms

The ultimate in convenience would be a separate bathroom for each bedroom. Such convenience is beyond the grasp of most of us, but shared baths, ingeniously planned, can be almost as useful.

If you have one bathroom out in the hall, serving two or more bedrooms, make the access to the bathroom as accommodating as possible. Lay a path of cozy carpeting or rugs for bare feet to pad along; eliminate obstacles to trip over; make sure the route is well lighted, with switches in handy locations.

The bathroom becomes much more private if you enter directly from the bedrooms instead of by walking along a corridor. A bath placed between two or more bedrooms, with a door opening to each bedroom, is an especially good arrangement for two children's rooms or a master bedroom and guest room.

Breaking a shared bathroom into compartments adds to its efficiency. The fixture most often isolated is the toilet. But why not put the tub in a separate compartment—then one person can enjoy an hour-long soak.

By duplicating some fixtures you can plan a bathroom in which some compartments are shared and others aren't. An extra sink, for example, frees the rest of the bathroom for someone else's use.

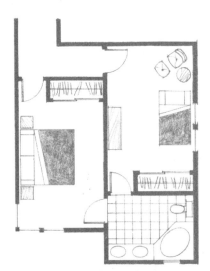

ENTRY to this family-only bathroom is through the bedrooms instead of from a much-traveled hallway.

BETWEEN TWO BEDROOMS, bathroom with fixtures in compartments lets two people share space.

Sharing some of the fixtures, but not all of them, adds convenience and still helps keep costs below the expense of entirely separate, complete bathrooms.

A private bathroom adjoining the bedroom

Second only to adequate clothes storage, a private connecting bathroom is the most wanted bedroom adjunct. Sometimes the bath opens to the bedroom through a door, but in other situations, the two rooms just flow together.

The transition between bed and bath may be through a dressing room or walk-in closet (see pages 72–78). Or a simple series of drawers or a dressing table, rather than a room, can form a link, providing visual and functional continuity between the spaces.

Planning a bathroom behind a partial wall or around a corner from the bed area can create a feeling of spaciousness with privacy.

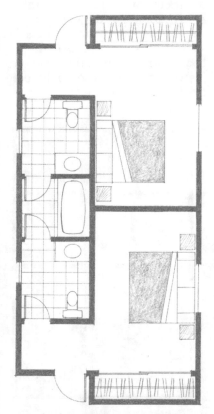

NEXT BEST THING to two separate bathrooms, extra sink and toilet make sharing a tub an easy compromise.

Fixtures in the bedroom

One or more elements usually found in a separate bathroom can go right into the bedroom, making the two rooms work as one. If you're remodeling, consider backing the new fixtures up to existing

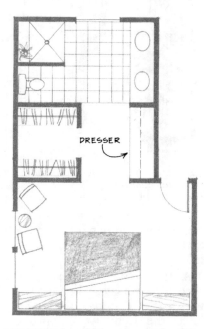

THE WALK from bedroom to bath takes you through a dressing area complete with walk-in closet.

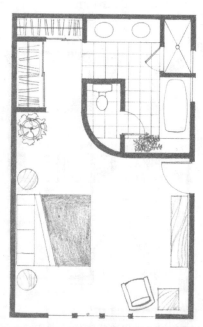

DESIGN UNIFIES three spaces—bedroom, dressing room, and bath—by means of curved wall and no doors.

plumbing—you may have a significant money saving. But on a new story or new section of the house, don't worry about where the existing plumbing is—any saving would be small in relation to the cost of the whole project.

Bringing in a sink

A bedroom sink simplifies tooth brushing and face washing, and if it's equipped with a well-lighted mirror, outlets for hair dryer and razor, and attractive storage, it will serve you bountifully. Since it's more visible than a sink in a separate bathroom, be sure it's good-

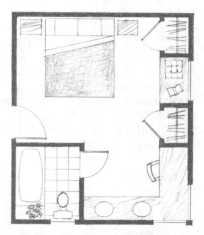

IN A MERGER of rooms, sinks are between the bed area and the rest of the bathroom.

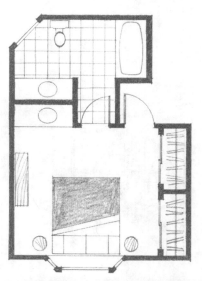

BACK-TO-BACK wash basins yield double accessibility when you want to brush teeth or wash hands in a hurry.

looking—a visual asset instead of a liability.

If you're planning two sinks anyway, putting one in the bedroom and the other in the bathroom, back to back, will avoid collisions during the morning rush hour.

A tub in the bedroom

Stepping from a warm bath directly into bed is a blissful way to wind up the day. Before you install a tub, though, you must take a cold, hard look at some practical considerations: the humidity and ventilation problems, and the extra weight of tub and water.

To disperse moisture, you can locate the tub next to an operable window or under an operable skylight. Should you choose to place the tub in the center of the room, you'll need to install a powerful fan to vent steam to the outside. Remember, too, that a tub in the middle of the room could be chilly; you may want a spot heater and perhaps a screen or curtain to shield you from drafts.

Regardless of location, you might consider putting the tub behind a glass wall. It would still be part of the bedroom visually, but the clouds of steam would be contained. You could plan a tub atrium, totally open to the sky or just well ventilated, putting moisture-laden air to work nurturing

ALMOST IN THE BEDROOM, this tub highlights an atrium. Glass keeps humidity in its place.

plants for a touch of green—or even a lavish garden—around the tub.

A tub, even a fiberglass one, is exceedingly heavy when it's filled with water. You may need to reinforce the floor to support the weight. Foundation requirements, along with plumbing, wiring, and ventilation needs, make it most practical to add a tub as part of a totally new bedroom.

Water-filled spas and hot tubs generate even more of a moisture problem than standard tubs that stand empty most of the time. It's really best to put such a tub outdoors if you're going to keep it full of water. In addition, the heating and filtering machinery are space-consuming and can be noisy. A deck or patio opening off the bedroom is an excellent location for a hot tub, and a nearby shower and dressing area make it ideal. (For more ideas, see the *Sunset* book *Ideas for Hot Tubs, Spas & Home Saunas.*)

Incorporating a shower or sauna in the bedroom

You have to close a door on a sauna, and a shower must be at least partially enclosed, though glass walls can be used for either. This makes them more difficult than other fixtures to position right in the bedroom. A shower requires plumbing connections and presents ventilation problems like a tub.

You can install a shower without including a sauna, but a sauna really requires a shower. You can convert a closet into a sauna by adding paneling and insulation, a bench, and a special door complete with heater, vent, light, controls, and window.

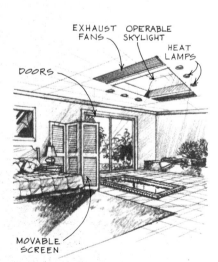

VENTILATION OPTIONS around a bedroom bathtub include doors to the outside, operable skylight, and vents.

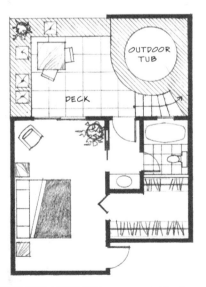

PUTTING A HOT TUB or spa outside the bedroom, rather than indoors, bypasses ventilation problems.

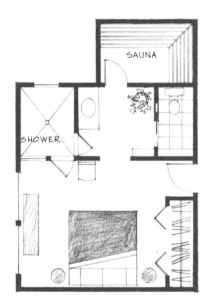

MORE THAN A STANDARD bedroom and bath combination, this one boasts a sauna and double-doored shower.

The tub's in the bedroom—almost. Dramatic mirrored divider with fireplace insert partially separates bedroom from bathroom. Buff-colored tile surrounds tub, then extends through to bedroom, forming a waterproof pathway and a hearth. Reflection shows antique armoire used for storing clothes.
Architect: Garrett Larsen.

With an open plan, two rooms combine into one

Clear glass of atrium opens view from bed in foreground past sink counter toward mirrored closet doors. Light streams down through slanting skylights—one with a sun-filtering lattice, the other a rolled-up shade. Straight through the atrium, behind the blind, is a sunken tub.
Architects: Backen, Arrigoni, and Ross.
Interior designer: Carol Barnes.

Design plus decoration links these rooms

Sleek, plastic-lacquered bed matches drawer fronts in dressing area that leads into bathroom (left). "Footboard" of bed is a chest of drawers. Carved-out walls, for window seat and lighted ledge (top photo), lend sculptural quality. Green fronds drape beam that runs across dressing area and entrance to bathroom. Skylights admit flood of natural light. Framed in wood, round mirror seems to float inside round window (springs attach it to window frame). Peppery carpeting and oak baseboards continue bedroom style into dressing area and bathroom.
Architect: Wendell Lovett.
Design consultant: Suzanne Braddock.

Twining flowers meander across wallpaper, bedspread, and draperies in adjoining bathroom and bedroom. Sink, faucets, and tile continue flower motif with perky blue blossoms. Style of skylight repeats small-paned design of windows beyond bed.
Architect: Michael Moyer.

Here the sink and dressing table are brought into the bedroom

Not-quite-twin mirrors at the sink/dressing table give off well-lighted reflections in paneled end of bedroom. Practical tile counter is easy to clean. Blue robe marks the well-placed closet. A pivot away from closet and sink, tub and toilet compartment displays same carpeting and use of redwood as the rest of the bedroom. Medicine cabinet is built into wall to left of sink.
Architect: Glenn B. Pollock.

Platform bed puts you on a pedestal

Thick, woolly carpeting to wiggle your toes in could make this platform a cold-morning delight. Or you could upholster it in smooth polished cotton in bright tropical colors for a totally different effect. The pedestal underneath the platform is barely visible, but you can upholster it to match, if you wish, and add a coordinated bedspread.

Thanks to the platform extensions, you won't need bedside tables or chairs (though as a sitting spot, the platform is probably nearer the floor than you're used to). The extensions around three sides create a continuous shelf.

This simple platform is designed to hold a queen-size (60" by 80") mattress at a comfortable height, with room to spare around the edges for lamps, books, or seating. Of course, you can modify it to hold any size mattress. Just be sure the platform doesn't overhang the support base by much more than 9".

Build the base first, from 2 by 10 lumber. Join the ends to the sides with ⅜" by 4½" lag bolts; drill holes before inserting the lag bolts, which are assembled with flat washers under the heads. Then use lag bolts to secure the center board.

Lay two sheets of ¾" plywood across the base, flush along the end that will be the head of the bed. Position the joint between the two sheets over the center board of the base. Screw the two sheets to the base with #8 by 1½" flat wood screws. Be sure to drill pilot holes and countersink the heads.

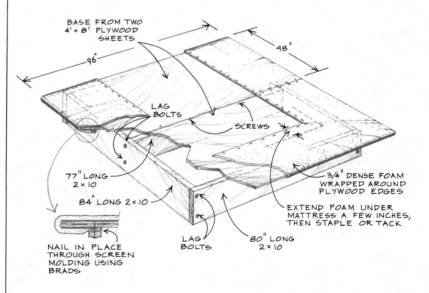

BASE FROM TWO 4' × 8' PLYWOOD SHEETS

96"

48"

LAG BOLTS

SCREWS

77" LONG 2 × 10

84" LONG 2 × 10

¾" DENSE FOAM WRAPPED AROUND PLYWOOD EDGES

EXTEND FOAM UNDER MATTRESS A FEW INCHES, THEN STAPLE OR TACK

LAG BOLTS

80" LONG 2 × 10

NAIL IN PLACE THROUGH SCREEN MOLDING USING BRADS

Now add the padding. For this, wrap ¾" dense foam around the edges of the platform, fastening it along the underside with cleats of screen molding and brads. Extend the foam across the platform surface and thumbtack or staple it where the mattress will conceal the staples or tacks.

Cover the foam with carpeting or a fabric that complements your bedspread. Carefully wrap and thumbtack or staple the carpeting or fabric in place.

Bedroom Decks, Windows & Skylights

Open the bedroom to starlight, fresh air, and early morning dew

Before the age of air conditioning, the sleeping porch was a favorite way to mesh the night outside with the privacy of the house. The same idea can be incorporated into the most modern dwelling to achieve energy-conserving natural temperature modification and lighting, as well as an esthetically pleasing setting.

Short of building a sleeping porch, you can open the bedroom to the outdoors with windows, skylights, decks, and patios. Opening up the bedroom allows a more dramatic use of space and relieves a boxed-in feeling.

What's outside?

The qualities of nature—moonlight and starlight, changing weather and seasons, cooling breezes, flowers and trees, pleasant views—add a whole new dimension to a sleeping room.

On the other hand, you may decide you want to screen out the exterior world, not let it in. Traffic noise, barking dogs, midsummer heat, or objectionable neighbors are all obstacles to a good night's rest.

Think carefully about what is outside a potential bedroom site. The most important aspect of a bedroom is its success as a setting for slumber. Listen to night sounds: serenading bullfrogs may lull you gently to sleep, but make your spouse toss and turn.

If you're building a new house, you might visit the site at night before you build. Before remodeling your own house or interchanging rooms, spend some night time in the proposed bedroom. You may be surprised at what you notice. For example, one side of the house might be at the crest of a hill, and the bedrooms here would be sunny and subject to noisy, buffeting winds. On the other side of the same house a stand of trees might cause bedrooms to be dark and cool all the year around.

Think also about how a room may change in a few months. A bedroom that's delightful in the summer may chill your toes when there's snow on the ground.

Start with a snug house

Designing your bedroom (and your entire house) with climate in mind lets you appreciate the conditions outside without wasting fuel fighting them.

Keep in mind that heat enters and escapes through windows, skylights, and doors. Especially if they're single-glazed, windows and skylights lose a substantial amount of heat per square foot. Proper insulation, weatherstripping, caulking, and storm doors and windows (or double or triple-glazed panes) prevent winter heat loss and summer heat gain.

Properly done, opening up the bedroom can actually save energy

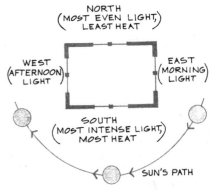

PICK THE POINT of the compass that suits your waking and sleeping patterns when adding a window or skylight.

by providing natural light and natural heating and cooling. Consult an architect or designer who is experienced in designing with nature to achieve the most economical results.

Restrictions have entered the building codes in the interest of conserving energy. Some of these guidelines can be strictly interpreted by building inspectors. In dealing with specific amounts of glass, you should rely on an architect or engineer to calculate the energy efficiency necessary to comply with the building code.

Think through cross-ventilation, while you're in the design stage, because the heavy insulation that's often used for energy conservation can make the bedroom stuffy.

Using the sun's light & warmth

Your own preference for morning or evening light (or lack of either), and the amount of daylight you prefer, will help determine the

BOUNCED DAYLIGHT sheds an even, overall illumination throughout the room; curved wall softens pattern.

amount and placement of glass or acrylic in your bedroom.

If you would like an awareness of light without direct sun, use high openings such as skylights or clerestory windows to let light wash over the walls. Natural light should be bounced—reflected off room surfaces—rather than allowed to shine directly into your eyes. Bring in light high on one wall so it will bounce off an opposite wall. The surface it hits can be white or a light color for an airy feeling, dark for a subdued, diffused effect.

There's another good reason to bounce sunlight: your bedspread, pillows, upholstery, and curtains won't fade as rapidly as in strong, direct sun.

Early risers in the northern hemisphere favor the morning light that comes from the east or southeast. Openings along an east wall offer direct morning sun; if they're overhead or high up on the wall you can bounce wake-up lighting. East-facing openings will transmit early-morning warmth into a bedroom, but in winter, heat will escape through them.

With openings facing the west or southwest you can watch the colors change as the sun sets. To enjoy long evenings, use openings on this side of the house; you may want to add shades, though, to lessen heat gain on hot days.

The warmest, most intense light comes from the south. Deciduous plantings outside the bedroom help block summer sun and admit winter rays. The greater the proportion of wall and roof area that faces south, and the more directly south it faces, the more heat the bedroom will capture from the winter sun.

When a bedroom doubles as an office or work room, you may prefer even, glare-free north light. Openings to the north won't offer much warmth, but they will provide gentle illumination.

Bedroom decks & patios

No matter what your taste—a Continental breakfast of café au lait and croissants alfresco, an hour-a-day sunbath, or a peaceful spot to relax and watch stars appear and listen to crickets chirp—you can enjoy it on a deck or patio adjacent to your bedroom.

Both decks and patios act as outdoor room extensions, creating separate, private spaces for every family member. In crowded cities or on steep hillsides, decks may be one way to capture scarce outside space. A bedroom deck or patio might be the perfect secluded location for a spa or hot tub (see photograph on page 51).

Sliding or hinged glass doors provide access, and they function like large windows, bringing in views, ventilation, and light.

Even if it's too tiny to sit on, a patio or deck can become a landscape painting—an attractive composition to be viewed and admired from the bedroom. Adding seasonal changes, such as flowers, fruit, or fall color, will keep it interesting. With fences, walls, and hedges you can create a verdant view with privacy.

If you plan to use furniture on a bedroom deck or patio, consider indoor-outdoor designs that could be utilized inside the bedroom during a summer shower or throughout the winter. Canvas, wicker, and aluminum styles are

INDOOR-OUTDOOR FURNITURE travels onto the patio for sunny days, returns to the bedroom when it rains.

lightweight, durable, and versatile. Cushions that pad built-in seating are easy to carry indoors for use as floor pillows.

Planning bedroom windows

Views, ventilation, light—one or all of these benefits come when you add windows to your bedroom. Another improvement is possible: windows on a bedroom wall that faces directly south become winter heat boosters. On a clear winter's day, the low sun's rays shine deeply into the room, warming the interior through a process called "the greenhouse effect" (for more information, see the *Sunset* book *Solar Heating & Cooling*).

Fixed windows (ones that don't open) are good heat conservers. But don't use them exclusively—be sure to allow for cross-ventilation and summer cooling.

Locate windows where you can enjoy them from the bed or, if you prefer, from elsewhere in the bedroom. Sill heights can be based on the furniture arrangement you have in mind (see pages 7–13). If you want privacy without giving up daylight or ventilation, consider putting windows high on the wall, an arrangement that also gives you more wall space for furniture.

Rather than popping in a single window, consider using a group. Grouped windows give more even light than separated ones, and also present a unified appearance. A window seat to curl up on or a greenhouse window for your African violet collection may be your idea of an idyllic alteration.

While you're window-dreaming, though, don't forget the exterior of your house. Adding windows to a bedroom will certainly change the way the house appears from outside.

The amount and kind of glass you use in windows is subject to building code restrictions. Tempered glass for safety or double glazing for energy efficiency may be mandatory. Other kinds of glass are used for decorative reasons—beveled or stained glass, for example. Window manufacturers will be happy to supply descriptions of the many available styles.

Window treatment choices—from billowy balloon shades to no-nonsense black-out curtains—are restricted only by your imagination and privacy and sun-control needs. If you plan to sew your own, let the *Sunset* book *Curtains, Draperies & Shades* help you. To stitch a coordinated bedroom ensemble, consult another *Sunset* book, *Slipcovers & Bedspreads*.

Louvers, shutters, and blinds, as well as stationary screens or café curtains, make good window treatments for bedrooms where privacy is a problem. You could also consider colored or mirrored glass, or a sheet of solar-reflective film that lets you see out but reflects on the outside during the day.

Should you add a skylight?

Since ceilings are such an important part of a bedroom—we're more aware of them there than in other rooms—you may want to add the extra dimension of a skylight. Skylights contribute visual drama as well as light and—with clear acrylic—views. Some skylights open to provide ventilation as well.

A small skylight can illumine a corner of the room, perhaps where you dress; a large one will diffuse daylight throughout the room. You might enjoy a luminous skylight, an installation that's a skylight by day and a section of glowing ceiling at night.

When you're positioning a skylight, make sure the sun won't shine directly into your eyes; shaft angles can be adjusted to direct sunbeams where you choose. If the sun is too intense, consider using translucent acrylic to reduce glare, or try a built-in shutter or insulated double domes. You could also block light as you would on a window, with horizontal shades or shutters.

Two potential skylight pitfalls are leaks and difficulty in cleaning. When installing a skylight, be careful that flashing and sealing are adequate. Rain washes skylights clean in some situations; in other cases, roof debris isn't visible from the room below. Most cleaning problems can be tackled with a long ladder and a hose or broom.

CLUSTERED WINDOWS, all of the same style, present a united front, allow sunlight to stream into the bedroom.

ANGLE A SKYLIGHT to enjoy maximum daylight without worrying about sun shining directly into your eyes.

Happy hot-tubbers enjoy redwood deck built off a bedroom. Deck continues around the corner
to the left, where there's glass behind the closed blind. Outdoor lighting makes the deck
and tub as usable at night as during the day.
Architect: Terry Mechling.

Extend to the out-of-doors with a bedroom deck or patio

In this merger of indoors and outdoors,
patio and bedroom join through sliding
glass doors. Overhead, patio has removable
plastic panels; bedroom enjoys circular
skylight. Color of bedroom carpeting
complements brick of patio.
Architect: Gene Henning.

Decks, Windows, Skylights **51**

Bringing in a view: windows brighten the bedroom

Leading the eye upward, windows and skylights stretch from floor to ceiling. Bay expands view from the bed. Branching oak trees form green curtain outside; no draperies are necessary.

More natural light travels across bedroom from windows at left. See-through, freestanding headboard/room divider lets daylight reach the wash basin and dressing area.
Architects: Backen, Arrigoni, and Ross.
Interior designer: Jean Hale.

Arches and arcs of glass turn windows into a graceful focal point. The three small-paned window sections swing open; the others are stationary. Bed platform extends to form a sitting ledge. Above the head of the bed, an interior window brings daylight into the dressing area.
Architect: William B. Remick.   Interior designer: Judith C. Oken.

Like the dot on an "i," round window rises above tall rectangular one. On the same wall, sliding glass door leads into garden. More glass—a stained glass panel rich with blue, green, and yellow—is above antique sewing machine cabinet at left. Architect: John Anderson.

Row of sky-turned windows runs all the way along one wall of upstairs bedroom. Plants sitting along ledge below windows thrive in the natural light. Architects: Noyola and Abels.

By moving a wood panel along its barn-door hardware, she opens interior window to let bedroom share daylight from other parts of the house. More daylight enters room from wood-framed skylights behind headboard. Architect: Garrett Larsen.

More than skylights: here are ways to flood the room with sun

Modern version of the old lightwell idea, this two-story light-bringer has glass on two sides and overhead. Adjustable blinds temper strength of daylight. From the bedroom, view is over the balcony to dense green of trees outside. Architect: Jay A. Fulton.

Light streams in through sliding glass doors, fixed-glass window, interior window, clerestories, and skylights. The interior window brings in more than daylight—firelight, moonlight, and music drift up from downstairs. This bedroom expansion included a small triangular deck, the right size for a few container plants and a chair. Roman shade on sliding glass doors, roller shade on clerestory window reduce glare; back of roller shade is laminated to protect fabric from fading. Architect: James Caldwell.

Bedside boxes stack high or low

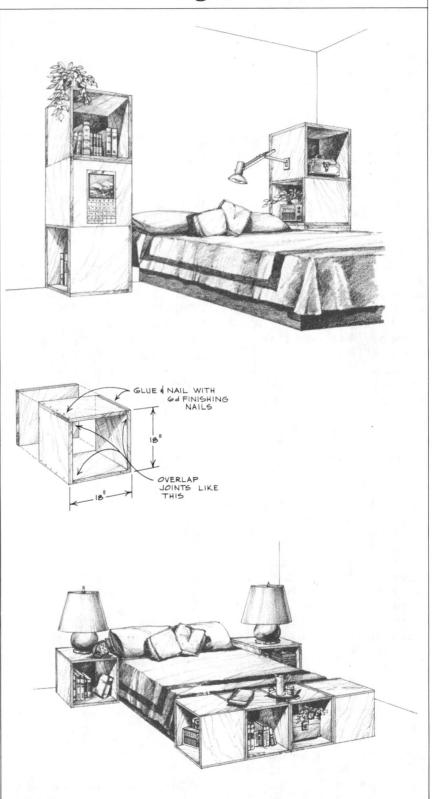

GLUE & NAIL WITH 6d FINISHING NAILS

18"

18"

OVERLAP JOINTS LIKE THIS

Simple wooden boxes—that's all you have to build to create this contemporary set of modular bedside cubes. Directions are given for a set of six boxes, stacked three high on each side of the bed. By building six you can lay a light bridge (described on page 63) across the boxes at the head of the bed at a good height for reading.

You can vary the number and arrangement of boxes to suit your bedroom. The set-ups shown offer out-of-view storage, bedside convenience, and a bit of display. Single cubes—one on each side of the bed—are the right height to serve as nightstands.

Build the set of six identical boxes out of high-quality ¾" plywood, cut with the best side outward. The *sides* of the boxes are identical pieces, each measuring 17¼" by 17¼". Cut twenty-four pieces. Cut six *back* pieces, each measuring 18" by 18".

Glue and nail together the box sides, using 6d finishing nails. Form the corners as shown in the drawing. Glue and nail the backs in place, making sure they are flush around all edges.

Set the nail heads below the surface, then fill the nail holes so they're flush with the surface; fill plywood edges also. Sand where necessary. Wipe off dust and paint the boxes with enamel.

If you prefer, you can cover the bedside boxes with wallpaper or fabric instead of painting them. Fabric stapled over a layer of batting will give an upholstered effect.

Ideas for Bedroom Lighting

Let the lights gleam, glint, and glow after the sun goes down

After the sun goes down, lighting becomes necessary—overall lighting so you can see the other end of the room, bedside lighting to read by, and ambient or mood lighting to cast an attractive glow for special effects.

Trained lighting consultants offer assistance in planning bedroom lighting, taking into consideration such factors as bedroom dimensions and color schemes. Typical lighting consultants are architects or interior designers who have made a specialty of studying illumination.

Lighting shops sell fixtures, but usually don't design lighting. Sometimes design advice is available (check the shop's advertising), but most often service is limited to help with choosing between specific brands and fixtures after the extent and placement of lighting have been determined. Generally, store personnel do not visit your home— but you can, of course, take plans into the lighting shops.

In illumination planning, it's important to remember that light surfaces reflect light and dark surfaces absorb it (exceptions are very shiny, lacquerlike finishes). Fabric textures also respond to light— such as the sheen of silk or the haze of mohair. Colors used in a room help determine the way

it should be illuminated: a bedroom's red rug may make the blue white effect of incandescent lighting desirable to cool the intense color.

About light bulbs. For any of the three types of lighting (overall, bedside, or mood), incandescent bulbs are best. Though fluorescent tubes use less energy than incandescents, they tend to dis-

MIRROR REFLECTS glow to the other end of the bedroom from these thoughtfully placed light fixtures.

tort colors and skin tones. Incandescent bulbs come in soft white, pink, and other flattering colors.

The type of bulb you use may be restricted by the structure of the light fixture. If the bulb socket swivels or points downward, you can use a reflector bulb; if the socket points upward, a standard incandescent bulb is required.

Saving energy. To cut your electric bill, consider reflector bulbs or fluorescent fixtures. Reflector bulbs, which are partially silvered inside, require about half as much wattage as standard incandescent bulbs. And using dimmers can conserve up to 30 percent of electricity.

Overall bedroom lighting

Bright (but not too bright) and well-distributed, shadow-free lighting is the goal in overall bedroom illumination. Plan this functional lighting first, then move on to bedside and mood lighting (though you may use some fixtures for more than one lighting purpose).

Keep in mind that the most important part of a lighting design is positioning; the strength of each individual bulb is secondary.

Be careful not to overtax existing wiring: if you must rewire to improve your lighting, you may want to consult the *Sunset* book *Basic Home Wiring Illustrated.*

The most common, but hardly the most effective, source of overall bedroom lighting is a central ceiling fixture. But any time you step between the light source and something you're trying to see, you cast a shadow. When you reach into a dresser drawer with your back to the light fixture, you'll throw a shadow right on your blue, black, and brown socks—hard enough to tell apart in broad daylight. Also, if you stand between a light source and a window you'll be silhouetted for neighbors and passers-by.

A better plan for overall lighting is to use wall fixtures or place lights on the perimeter of the ceiling.

Dual switch controls keep you from having to stumble around a darkened bedroom in search of a light. Placing one switch by the door to the room and another next to the bed is more convenient, and avoids wasted motion and possible collisions.

If it's on dimmer controls, your overall lighting can also be used for mood lighting. The bright get-dressed-and-brush-your-teeth light can be subdued with the twist of a knob.

Track lights are also useful for both overall and mood effects. They can spotlight an indoor plant or bounce light off the ceiling for room-filling illumination. Part of the usefulness of track lights is lost if they can't be adjusted; position them where you can reach them by standing on a bed or on a stepladder.

Bedside lighting

A light source you can reach from bed is a virtual necessity. As long as switches are within arm's reach, the fixture can be inset in the ceiling, attached to the wall next to or behind the bed, placed on an adjacent table, or built into the headboard or frame. One fixture to avoid is a high intensity lamp that sheds glaring, too-strong light. Unshielded or bare bulbs are also not desirable.

Don't make the mistake of leaving the bedroom entirely dark except for bedside light: too much

contrast is hard on the eyes. The most convenient arrangement is to be able to reach all light switches—for lights elsewhere in the bedroom as well as controls for your bedside lamp—without getting out of bed.

Adjustable lamps are, in many people's opinion, the best for in-bed reading. Whether you sit bolt upright turning pages as fast as you can to find out "whodunit," or recline to court sleep with a volume of poetry, an adjustable lamp can turn and tilt with you. And with an adjustable light, one person can read until 2 A.M. without disturbing a bed partner.

Adjustable lighting includes track lights, clamp-on drafting lamps that can be moved easily, goose-neck lamps, and swinging wall-mounted lights.

If you prefer a nonadjustable lamp with a shade, place it so the lower edge of the shade is at eye level while you're in an angle of repose. The lamp should be about 22 inches away from your bed. Adjustable or not, reading light should be directed onto the page from the side, not from overhead.

Table lamps with heavy bases and easy-to-operate switches are

FOR CONVENIENCE, place switches that control the central light fixtures by the bedroom door and beside the bed.

PORTABLE OR PERMANENT, adjustable lamps provide a very versatile type of bedside lighting.

HIDDEN BEHIND A VALANCE, lights along the edge of the ceiling wash two walls with a balanced brightness.

less likely to be knocked over than delicate ones with cleverly hidden controls.

Lighting for special effects

You can mingle light and shadow to create the effect you want: If you want to draw attention to one area of the room, concentrate light there. Fixtures that run the length of a wall wash the surface with even light, either soft or bright. A pool of light in an otherwise shadowy room creates a cozy place to sit. Generally, subdued light is relaxing; juxtaposition of light and shadow is dramatic.

Try focusing light on a favorite object, such as a painting or plant you especially enjoy. Picture lights can be installed on the wall or on the frame. Or you can create an impact with the tight oval of light cast by a spotlight. Floodlights are another possibility—they work like spotlights except that they radiate a wider beam of more diffused light. A picture in a rectangular frame can be outlined with a rectangle of light cast by a projector lamp.

Objects on a shelf can be illuminated by an unobtrusive fixture fastened to the underside of an overhanging shelf. To deliberately show off the light fixture, place it on the shelf.

Illuminate a large house plant or other major object by setting lights on the floor so they shine upward.

Mood lighting doesn't have to be electrical; candles and gas lanterns make attractive alternatives.

As with overall lighting, the fastest and easiest way to adjust your room's mood lighting is with dimmers.

Special-effect lighting works closely with room decoration. Mirrors and shiny surfaces multiply light sources and add drama. Reflection also makes it harder to discern boundaries—the room seems larger than it really is. Colored light bulbs and lamp shades will lend a special look to bedroom areas.

Select a special effect

LIGHT BECKONS THE EYE to a picture arrangement or other point of interest that you might like to emphasize.

FOCUSING LIGHT on a furniture grouping creates an island of brightness in an otherwise dark bedroom.

POINT THE LIGHT upward instead of down to bring new drama–shadows and ceiling interest–into a bedroom.

TAKE YOUR CHOICE between all-but-invisible lighting units that attach to shelves, and fixtures as display.

Overhead interest emphasized by lighting

Candles add atmosphere to bedroom that's lighted by three small-scale lights on a track. In remodeling, ceiling was opened to add height to bedroom, reveal shape of hip roof, and provide extra dimension of open joists. Insulation, gypsum wallboard, and paint are new. Cord for lights is virtually invisible—it runs on top of joist, then down wall to electrical outlet. Architect: Pamela M. Seifert.

Washed with light, gray white stained cedar walls and angled ceiling expand illumination from the two overhead lights. This small bedroom has a corner of glass (behind leafy *Ficus benjamina*) that reflects the flickering candles. Architect: Gene Henning.

Worthy of an art gallery, lighting shows off the major oil painting on the right-hand wall and the arrangement of smaller works around the bed. Two lights inset into ceiling direct attention to the large canvas while illuminating the bedroom as a whole. The wall-wide soffit and cabinetry form strong horizontal elements at the head of the bed.
Architect: Andrew Belschner of Robinson, Mills, & Williams.

Here the overall lighting is unusual

Directed upward, lights built into ledge ring the bedroom. In remodeling, old ceiling was removed to reach into attic. Molding in keeping with the house style was added to new curved ceiling. Rheostatted lights play up the molding and draw attention to ceiling shape.
Architect: Thaddeus E. Kusmierski.
Headboard design: Ron Newman.

Under the overhang, sleeping quarters offer a surprisingly cozy appeal for such an open arrangement. The warmth of the diagonally paneled wall contributes to this effect, as does the lighting: track lights above the bed, a table lamp for reading, and lights accenting the top of the overhang.
Architect: William Arthur Patrick.

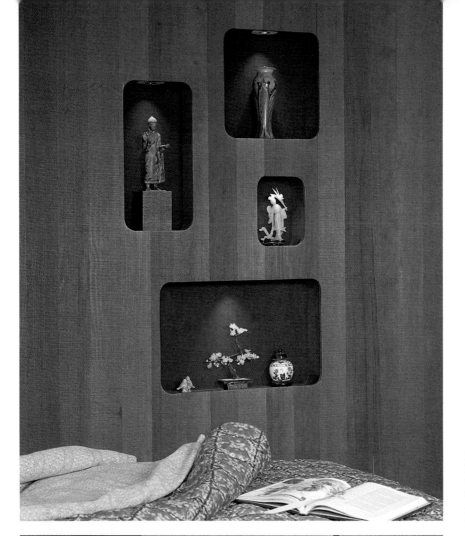

Localized lighting accents favorite objects

Each velvet-lined art niche boasts its own light. A most effective display method, the different-size wall cutouts create a lovely focal point in the bedroom.
Architect: Mogens Mogensen.
Interior designer: Alan Lucas.

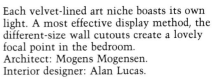

Shelves full of favorite things are emphasized by hidden fluorescent tubes that shed light downward from the top of the "headboard." In addition, two wall lamps provide reading light.
Architect: William Arthur Patrick.

Lights bridge the head of the bed

This bridgelike structure, which creates a semi-enclosed alcove at the head of the bed, is designed to accompany the set of bedside boxes described on page 55. The light bridge requires the support of the boxes or of some other similar structure.

This light bridge is basically a long box constructed of 1 by 10 boards and ¼″ perforated hardboard, with two recessed light fixtures. The light fixtures, designed for installation in ceilings, are sold in lighting stores. The ones shown are only 7¼″ high. We suggest eyeball-type trim for best directional control of the light. Each light is wired to a standard cord that plugs into a wall receptacle; you add a switch to each cord.

All parts of the long box are made of 1 by 10 boards except the back, which is ¼″ perforated hardboard (for ventilation). To figure the proper light bridge length for your bed, measure the bed's width and add 40″ (18″ for each set of bedside boxes plus an extra 2″ clearance on each side for blankets). Use this measurement as the cut length for the front and back pieces. Cut the front piece from 1 by 10 lumber; cut the back piece the same length and 9¼″ wide from perforated hardboard. Cut the top and bottom pieces 1½″ shorter. Cut two 9¼″-long pieces for the sides.

Before assembling the box, buy the recessed lights. Measure their diameter and check the manufacturer's instructions for proper clearances and hole sizes. For the type shown, you need a 6⅝″ hole; change this dimension if necessary.

Cut circular holes for the recessed fixtures in the bottom 1 by 10 (center the holes over each half of the bed). If the light fixtures have adjustable joist hangers, re-

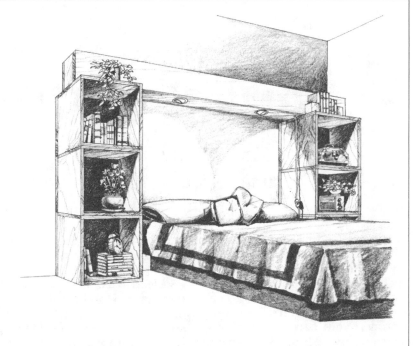

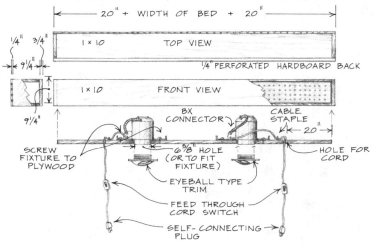

move them. Screw the fixtures in place with ¾″ screws. Drill small holes for the cords and connect the fixtures to #16 lamp cords as shown. Be sure to allow for enough cord to reach the receptacles. Add feed-through switches and plugs (the self-connecting kind are easiest to install).

If the installation directions that come with the light fixtures are not sufficient, consult the *Sunset* book *Basic Home Wiring.*

Construct the rest of the box around the bottom piece. Using simple butt joints, fasten together all the wooden parts except the back with glue and 6d finishing nails. The side pieces overlap the top and bottom. Screw the back in place so it's easy to remove.

Set all nail heads. Fill holes and sand where needed. Wipe clean and paint with enamel. Set in place, making sure there's an air space behind the back.

Bedside Amenities

*Around the bed: Stack bedtime stories,
tune in late-night TV, unwind with music*

Eat, drink, and be merry ... sage advice that might just as well apply to your bedroom. By adding such amenities as television, music, books and magazines, a coffeepot, even a refrigerator to your bedside, you can transform a Spartan setting into a welcoming retreat.

A series of electrical outlets near the bed (or built into a bed frame) lets you add and subtract an electric blanket, clock radio, heating pad or hair dryer. With outlets hidden inside cabinets, small appliances can stay plugged in, ready to use yet out of sight at bedside.

A bedside phone has become fairly standard; to keep even more in touch with the outside world, you might want to add an intercom or controls to a house security system to your bedside.

For television addicts

Whether you start the day with an early-morning talk show or end it with a midnight movie, a bedroom television set lets you overlap TV viewing with your sleeping hours.

Television/clock combinations and tiny "belly tellies" are fine for close-range viewing. One of these small sets can be positioned on a bedside table and easily adjusted for the right viewing angle.

But adding a wide-screen television set takes a bit more planning. Unless you have an adjustable bed, a large console should be carefully located for best viewing from a reclining position. You might consider placing the television on a high shelf against the wall, or suspending it from the ceiling. You'll find additional ideas for locating your bedroom television set in the photographs on pages 22, 37, 54, 68, 70, and 75.

Though bedroom television sets are most often viewed from the bed, some people like to watch television while dressing or sitting in another part of the bed-

OVER-THE-BED TABLE—the easily moved type used in hospitals—can be rolled into your bedroom at home.

BRING THE WORLD to you, not vice versa, with bedside communication devices such as telephone or intercom.

room. A swiveling or pivoting TV stand makes it easy to change the orientation of the set from bed to easy chair.

LARGE SCREEN entertainment—best viewed in a large bedroom—re-creates the atmosphere of a movie theater.

For deliciously lazy TV viewing, you'll want to treat yourself to a set with remote controls.

With large video screens you can enjoy movielike effects while comfortably ensconced in bed. By adding equipment to tape television programs, you'll never have to miss your favorite show.

Planning for books & magazines

Some bedrooms are part library (see photographs on pages 35–37). But even with a book-lined bedroom sitting area, it's fun to read in bed occasionally. Bedside reading "musts" include good lighting (see page 57) and a place to store your reading material. A bedside table may be sufficient for some people; inveterate readers may find shelves to the ceiling barely adequate.

Here are some ideas to increase your storage space: Hang pocket-style or racklike book and maga-zine holders on a wall next to the bed or on the side of a piece of furniture within easy reach. Move freestanding magazine racks from the living room to the bedroom. Attach casters to a tray to roll your magazines underneath the bed, out of the way during the daytime.

For total relaxation while reading in bed, it's important to select well-designed, comfortable pillows. With this backrest in place, you might set your novel on a sloping book stand.

The sound of music

Stereo speakers, turntable, radio, and tape player make delightful additions to a bedroom. If you make your own kind of music, the bedroom can double as a practice room—a music stand takes up very little space.

Sound systems can be simple or elaborate. Radio/clock combinations that lull you to sleep on a wave of soft music, or wake you

TINY TV travels around the room with ease; you can move it from nightstand to top of the dresser.

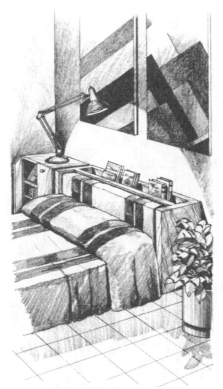

BEYOND THE BASIC BOOKSHELF, try keeping bedtime reading materials in a headboard or within the bed frame.

SOFT MELODIES to dream by or spirited tunes to wake up with—music brings an extra dimension to a bedroom.

with a melody instead of an alarming buzz, are inexpensive and familiar to most of us.

The owners of the bedroom pictured at the bottom of page 67 slide a portable tape player into a bedside drawer; the player can be used with or without headphones, and tapes and player can be moved from the bedroom to elsewhere in the house—or the car.

A more elaborate setup for sound is the partial wall pictured at the top of page 70. Concealed behind the grasscloth on either side of the television set are twin speakers. Cabinet doors on the other side of the wall open for access to the speaker workings. Controls for volume, balance, and tuning are in a console that sits next to the bed.

But rather than install separate music arrangements for the bedroom, you might prefer to bring in an extension speaker from the living room or family room, thereby saving the considerable price of duplicating the equipment.

A word about sound: Heavy bass beats seem to carry through almost anything. Soundproofing your bedroom with absorbent materials and adequate wall framing and insulation will keep most noise from disturbing the rest of the household.

Food & drink

If you want to return to your bedroom for a midmorning coffee break or share a light supper somewhere other than the kitchen or dining room, try setting up your bedroom for eating and drinking ease. The likelihood of your actually cooking in the bedroom is rather slim, but it's possible that you'll serve food and beverages there.

Depending on how many picnics in bed you enjoy, you could include outlets for a warming tray or a coffeepot, or plug in a toaster oven for cinnamon toast or warm bagels. A small refrigerator could be added, too, for a bedside supply of ice and chilled orange juice—or

cream cheese and lox to go with the bagels.

A bed frame can be designed to include surfaces for arranging appetizers or dessert (see the photograph at the top of page 67). A bedside table with a breadboard-type pullout, or simply one with plenty of surface area, could be used to set a tray on. If you plan to dine in the bedroom regularly, arrange chairs and a small table to use as a buffet.

Elegant accessories make any meal a delight. You might want to collect a variety of pretty dishes in settings for one or two. Put everything on a special wicker tray—and don't forget the flowers.

If you have a second-floor bedroom over a kitchen, pantry, or hall, you can bring up a freshly prepared feast via a dumbwaiter—and whisk away leftovers the same way. A more down-to-earth suggestion for a single-story house: wheel a serving cart from kitchen to bedroom. After all, the luxury of room service shouldn't be kept just for vacations.

WHEELING IN breakfast is the work of minutes if you use a serving cart. Don't forget a flower or two.

BEDROOM BANQUETING takes you away from the hubbub of the kitchen and the formality of the dining room.

WHY CLIMB STAIRS with a heavy tray when a dumbwaiter will bring a snack up to you? It's like having a butler.

Custom beds designed for bedside convenience

They're making the most of a big (9 by 10-foot) bed in a small (12 by 13-foot) room. Custom ¾-inch plywood frame has built-in box spring, stereo speakers, lights; it holds telephone, clock, and books. All wiring is enclosed within the carpeted plywood structure. Mattress with fitted quilted bedspread sits slightly higher than the platform bed.
Interior designer: William G. Gaylord.

Even the headboard opens on this bed and cabinetry combination. Pillows are stored behind the hinged headboard panels; books, clock, and small cylinder lights are on open shelf above bed. Four large drawers (each 9 by 30 by 35 inches) pull out from under bed. The open one stores headphone, tapes, even night-light; wires run through notch cut in back of drawer. Other drawers contain bedspread, blankets, clothes. Cabinets at sides of bed contain bookshelves and magazine rack.
Architect: Mark Mills.
Interior designer: Karen Hammond.

Stylish storage in specialized headboards

All the way to the ceiling, built-in headboard consists of shelves and convenient ledges. Window inset in headboard opens to a lightwell filled with potted plants. Fireplace was retained in remodeling of Edwardian row house. Architect: Jennifer Clements.

Headboard, room divider, side tables (see photo at right), and chest of drawers—all in one piece of furniture. Laminated plastic finish is easy to keep clean; clear acrylic pulls are unobtrusive. Pale wool over a layer of padding wraps the heavy boards that form bed base. On windows, vertical drapes use tiny dots to pick up subtle tones—taupe, beige, gray—of textured rug.

Sherbet-toned sheets look inviting, especially when you can settle in and have your tea within arm's reach. Handy shelf sits in pull-around drawer with curved edge. Cabinetry stretches along whole wall, includes tilt-up backrest. Designer: Richard Pennington.

Easy-to-reach side shelf sits lower than surface of bed. This side unit and its counterpart at other end of headboard (see photo at left) house clock-radio, electric blanket control, television remote control, telephone. Light switches and security system switches are built into headboard. Interior designer: Alan Lucas.

All set for late-night movies, a TV in the bedroom

Hinged to 6-foot-high freestanding wall, painting swings wide to reveal television. Inside wall, next to television, are stereo speakers; controls for both are at bedside. Architect: William W. Hedley, Jr. Interior designer: Charles Falls.

Niches for the television and for linens are concealed neatly behind folding louvered doors. Louvers match window shutters, ventilate the two niches and shelves below as well. Wall section was added during remodeling. Interior designer: Nadine Marchand Cardwell.

Water bed frame features compartments

Conceal your alarm clock or stow your slippers in the compartments at the head and foot of this waterbed frame. The compartments hinge on the outside edge, so they're easy to reach into from the bed.

The design shown is for a king-size water mattress that measures 6′ by 7′ (72″ by 84″).

First, cut the 2 by 10s for the frame to length. You'll need four at 73¼″ (A and B) and two at 118″ (C and D). Cut ½″ by ⅝″ dadoes along the lengths of (B), (C), and (D) to fit the ½″ plywood bottom (I). Cut 1½″ by ⅝″ dadoes and rabbets across (C) and (D) for receiving the (A) and (B) pieces. Be sure to cut the dadoes on the (C) piece so they are mirror images of (D) cuts.

Assemble the 2 by 10s flat on the floor to make sure they fit together properly. Counterbore and drill pilot holes for 4½″ by ½″ lag screws at the four corners (two per corner).

Now cut (best side to face outward) the compartment lids and bottoms (total of eight pieces) from ¾″ plywood: four for the foot of the bed (G) measuring 11⅞″ by 35⅞″ and four for the head of the bed (H) that are 15⅞″ by 35⅞″. Drill 1¼″ finger holes in the four lids (two of each size) or plan to add knobs after painting.

Cut the egg-crate-style support grid from ¾″ plywood. You'll need three pieces 83″ by 9″ (E) and three 60″ by 9″ (F). Cut ¾″ by 4½″ notches in each of these. Fill and sand all edges, then paint this support grid, the compartment lids, and—if you wish—the bed frame.

Cut two 36⁹⁄₁₆″ by 85⅛″ pieces (I) of ½″ plywood for the platform bottom. Sand the edges lightly and

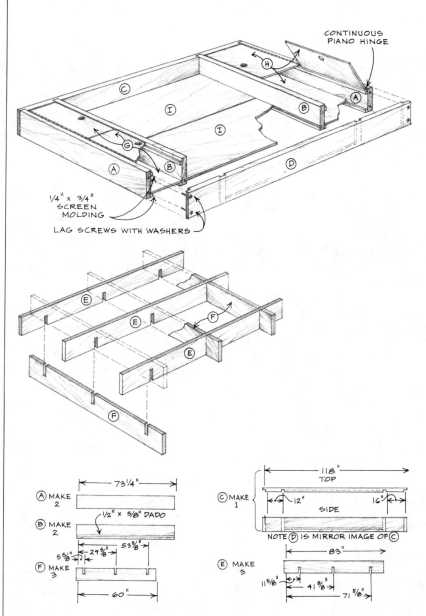

lay these on top of the assembled support grid. Now, get a helper to steady the grid, and lag screw the bed frame together around the platform.

Hinge the compartment lids in place as shown, using continuous

hinges. Nail the screen moldings where they belong to support the lids and the compartment bottoms. Drop the bottoms in place.

Touch up with paint where necessary. Add liner and water bed mattress.

Dressing Rooms & Closets

Tubs, bins, baskets, and drawers to keep your clothes composed

Everyone knows there's no such thing as enough closet space. It's one of those mysterious laws of modern life that no matter what you do to expand clothes storage space, your wardrobe expands slightly faster.

But don't despair. We've included storage ideas in this chapter to help keep things under control—even if you're struggling to pack clothes into a closet that's dark, minute, and stuffed to the ceiling. You'll find dressing room and closet ideas to suit a variety of situations, from apartment bedrooms where remodeling is impossible, to design ideas for completely renovated bedrooms.

Creating a closet

If you're adding a new bedroom or redesigning an existing one, you'll want to give some careful thought to the location of your clothes storage and dressing area. There are a number of possibilities.

Perhaps you'll want your closet/dressing room close to the bedroom door—a good arrangement for a small bedroom. Or a dressing room could be located next to an adjoining bathroom, thereby saving steps.

To augment a dresser, you might include a couple of drawers you can reach into for a sweater as you step out of the bedroom.

A walk-in closet neatly combines clothes storage and dressing space: the clothes storage wraps around the dressing area. About 3 feet of clear space allows ample room to dress between rows of hanging garments. You should allow a minimum depth of about 1½ feet for each row of hangers; 2 feet is preferable.

But even without structural changes in your bedroom, you can rethink your clothes storage area—simply rearrange the existing space. For example, you could make use of two small closets by separating your clothes—perhaps a winter closet and a summer one ... or an everyday closet and a dressy one.

Though built-ins take up the least space, separate pieces of furniture can be grouped to create a closet/dressing site. Such individual pieces may not be as suited to your wardrobe needs as custom built-ins, but they can be moved around as requirements change.

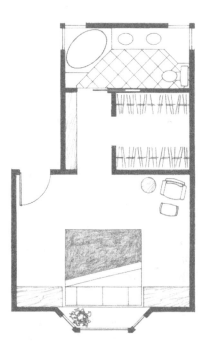

IF YOUR BATHROOM adjoins your bedroom, a good place for clothes storage might be a closet corridor.

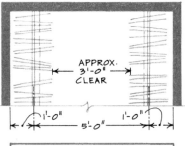

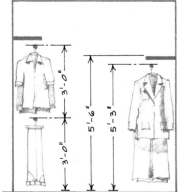

USE THESE DIMENSIONS to help plan a closet. The same allowance for hanging clothes is needed in any type of closet.

Divide & conquer

Machiavelli's famous phrase applies as aptly to clothes storage as to political planning. Though most people want more square feet of space in their closets, making more efficient use of the space you already have may be a better answer. Planning your closet, and its subdivisions, around your own wardrobe will customize it to use the space to best advantage. Take a look at your wardrobe to determine what you need.

First divide your wardrobe into full-length clothes that hang, those stored on shelves, and garments kept in drawers. Figure how much space is needed for each clothing category and then add 10 percent—the extra allows for new clothing purchases and for air circulation between garments.

Behind closed doors

With the possible exception of folding doors, most doors can be used for storage. Even with sliding doors, the outer panel is available for slim storage. Since this surface is always visible, the most practical use is for hanging attractive storage containers such as a basket for socks and other small items. A mirror can be hung on a reasonably sturdy sliding door, and a collection of pretty scarves or necklaces hung from pegs adds color to an informal bedroom.

With hinged doors, both the inner and outer surfaces can be used for storing clothes and accessories, especially if there is plenty of clearance between the door and the clothing inside. You can drape ties and trousers over towel bars, or tack up an attractive shoe bag or soft shelf system for storing shirts and sweaters. And you can hang almost anything if you have a panel of pegboard and the correct hardware.

Into the interior

Unused space is often lurking right inside the closet—above the clothes rod, below hanging clothing, and along the side walls.

Two clothes rods, one above the other, will double your hanging space. What if styles suddenly change, and hemlines are 6 inches longer than they were last year? You can keep your carefully subdivided closet from becoming obsolescent by planning ahead—by installing an adjustable clothes rod, adjustable shelves, or an easy-to-move spring rod.

By placing casters on a small chest of drawers, a set of shelves, or a cart made of hanging trays, you can roll folded clothes underneath clothing that hangs from a high rod.

Built-in shelves are a great boon, especially when they're sized to suit your needs. A stack of shirts and sweaters won't disappear into the depths of your closet if the

APPEALINGLY ORGANIZED closet has acrylic sweater boxes, hanging baskets, tidy shoe rack; shades conceal shelves.

THE OUTSIDE SURFACE of a closet door can be used for storage. Mirror, trays, and expandable hat rack decorate this one.

INSIDE THE CLOSET, space-saving storage might include pegboard, towel bars, and a shoe bag hung from the door.

PORTABLE SHELVES—a small furniture piece with casters—fit underneath clothes rod that holds hanging apparel.

shelves are shallow. If you already have deep shelves, install pull-out trays or put seldom-used things toward the back. Fabric shades will hide shelf disarray.

You could personalize your closet with special built-in compartments for shoes, purses, and hats, but sliding trays or baskets, acrylic boxes, and shoe bags and racks are readily available for those who prefer not to build in storage.

Dressing area/closet improvements

Some basics to consider in upgrading your dressing area include proper lighting, mirrors, space for clothes-care equipment, and the area's over-all appearance.

Good lighting where you dress and inside the closet helps you look your best. Natural light from a window or skylight (see pages 48–50 and the photographs on pages 51–54) will give you the truest idea of how your outfit will look in daylight. But don't let strong direct sun shine on clothes being stored—sunlight fades clothes and causes fibers to deteriorate over a period of time.

As well as illuminating, a window ventilates a stuffy closet or dressing area. Louvered doors also permit air circulation.

It's best to have a closet light operated on an independent switch. If your closet is too small for an interior light, try angling a bedroom light fixture toward the closet entrance.

Three-way, adjustable full-length mirrors are ideal for dressing areas, but a single full-length mirror will do nicely. Lighting in front of the mirror should be bright without casting shadows; the light should shine on you, not on the mirror.

For standing or moving-around room, allow enough floor space next to your clothes storage. A place to sit—whether it's a bench, chair, or the corner of the bed—makes dressing easier.

Equipment for care of your clothes—shoe polish, lint brush, spot remover, needle and thread, iron, portable steamer—can be kept in a dressing area and used there. Don't forget a clothes hamper or basket for laundry.

Putting the finishing touches on your closet and dressing area might include sprucing up walls, doors, and ceiling with paint or paper, and adding a toe-pleasing, nonslipping rug underfoot. You could continue the bedroom's color scheme or separate the dressing area of a large bedroom with a different decor.

Storage ideas from the past

Before the era of built-in closets, a bedroom wasn't complete without an armoire, matching bedstead, dressing table, and chest of drawers. The solid wood and craftsmanship found in these antiques still make them a good value for those who like the look of bedroom "separates."

If you need an additional closet, consider an armoire built prior to 1900, since such armoires are usually deep enough to hold a clothes rod run horizontally. More shallow armoires can be fitted with hooks or with rods that run from front to back. When you shop, take a tape measure with you to check the depth and also the height—some armoires were designed for rooms with high ceilings, so may be too high for your room.

Armoires with drawers, shelves, and cabinets all in one piece of furniture are called fitted wardrobes. Combining different types of storage space, these wardrobes can be thought of as the original wall system. Primarily of English origin, fitted wardrobes are known as "doubles" or "triples," depending upon the number of furniture pieces they combine. They take up less space than separate pieces of furniture, and may come apart for ease in moving.

A linen press—a combination of cabinet top with drawers below—is adaptable for bedroom use. If you don't especially need the lipped shelves behind the cabinet doors, you could hide a television set in the cabinet top.

A sideboard, with a mirror above and drawers and cabinets below, can be at home in a bedroom as well as in a dining room.

Another very popular piece of antique bedroom furniture is the cheval glass, a full-length, tilting mirror on a stand.

A FEW OF THE ANTIQUES you might add to a modern bedroom are a fitted wardrobe, linen press, cheval glass.

DRESSING ROOM that has everything includes a full-length mirror, a bench to sit on, and good lighting and ventilation.

Closets constructed within a bedroom

Selecting an outfit seems easier with this well-divided wall of storage. Adding the 20-inch-deep closet ate up floor space but made small bedroom more efficient—no inches are wasted. Cabinetry detail matches bedroom door, other trim throughout house. Pull-out, swiveling television can be watched from bed. Interior designer: Joan Papathakis.

Parallel curtains slide along ceiling tracks, a type of hardware originally used in hospitals. Solid-blue fabric closet "door" takes up very little space. Print curtain creates a bed enclosure. Architect: Peter W. Behn.

Warm tones of oak plywood extend along entire wall. Walk-in closet is supplemented by generous drawers and cabinets on wall. Overhead light panels just inside door illuminate closet; mirrored door reflects the light. Architect: Mark Mills. Interior designer: Karen Hammond.

Golden-hued dressing room (left) echoes design of the bedroom (above) with wood-trimmed white walls, soft brown carpeting, finely detailed wood ceiling. Clear skylight and track lights illuminate clothing colors. Shoe cubbyholes are in cabinet with door ajar; clothes hang behind double doors (see floor plan). Architect: Charles L. Howell.

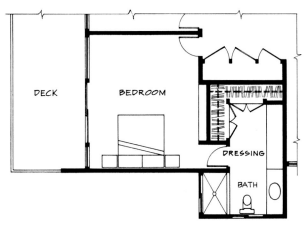

The idea's the same

Nostalgia from antiques in oak, the wall light, and a clock enhances this bedroom corner. Clothing and linens are easy to see in glass-doored dry goods cabinet set into wall. Architect: John Anderson.

set apart from the bed

Mirrored closet doors add dimension to this dressing corridor. Window brings in natural light; vertical drapes ensure privacy. Freestanding wall at left has drawers for clothes, divides dressing area from rest of bedroom (see page 70).
Architect: William W. Hedley, Jr.
Interior designer: Charles Falls.

Translucent skylight overhead brings true daylight into this walk-in closet. Shelves and slanted drawers supplement clothes rods. Adjacent bathroom has similar skylight; blue carpeting extends into bedroom. Architect: Michael Moyer.

—built-in compartments for clothes

Contemporary, crisp lines and primary colors delight the eye in this thoughtfully detailed bedroom. Storage unit is set flush with bedroom wall, but extends out to add exterior form to house.
Architect: Wendell Lovett.

See-through drawers in rounded room divider let clothing colors add interest to room. Bed platform cantilevers out from step-up drawers; twin skylights brighten bed area.

Looking past rounded divider toward bathroom, mirror reflects ties hung on dowels. Architect: Gary Allen.

The bathroom-dressing room link

In the foreground is one of a pair of sinks, conveniently placed in the corridor leading to a generous closet. Interior clerestories open to skylighted stairwell; bedroom is on other side of stairwell. Within the walk-in closet, stacked coated-wire baskets keep clothing visible and organized. Rods at varying heights divide clothing of different lengths; shelves utilize rest of closet. Architect: William J. Zimmerman.

A basin in the dressing room—especially one with a hand-held sprayer—is a great convenience. This one's in a grooming area bright with windows and a skylight. Closet has built-in dresser facing hanging clothes. Bedroom is to left, beyond built-in dresser. Architect: Kirby Ward Fitzpatrick.

Organizer: in a closet or on its own

With this organizer or your own variation on the theme, you can tap unused closet space. Slipped into an existing closet, it will divide and display your clothes without wasting a centimeter. Or it can be used as a freestanding piece of furniture with a curtain concealing what's stored.

If you plan to install this closet organizer inside an existing closet, figure the organizer's height and width so that once it's assembled, you can position it inside the closet easily. On the other hand, if you will use it as a freestanding closet, make it about 7' tall and a width to meet your requirements.

Be sure to take standard curtain sizes into consideration if you don't plan to sew your own. And remember that if the boxes are spaced more than 3' apart, the closet poles may need intermediate support.

Map out the three tall boxes. The width of each box depends on how you plan to use it. If you want to build in shelves, the width is up to you. But if you intend to install wire baskets or plastic bins as drawers, buy the baskets or bins and build to fit them. Be sure to allow enough clearance for runners—we suggest using U-shaped aluminum channels as drawer runners, but you can substitute wooden molding.

The boxes, shelves, and top are made from ¾" plywood. (For the backs of the boxes, you can use ¼" plywood, if you wish.) Work from an overall plan. Sketch out the dimensions, referring to the clearances suggested in the drawing. Figure number and location of drawers and shelves.

When you're ready, cut all the pieces except the long shelves and

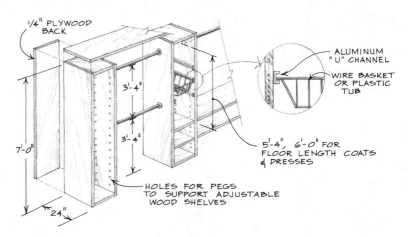

¼" PLYWOOD BACK

7'-0"

3'-4"

3'-4"

24"

ALUMINUM "U" CHANNEL

WIRE BASKET OR PLASTIC TUB

5'-4", 6'-0" FOR FLOOR LENGTH COATS & DRESSES

HOLES FOR PEGS TO SUPPORT ADJUSTABLE WOOD SHELVES

closet poles. Always cut with the best side of the plywood outward. Note that if the unit will be installed in a closet, the top should fit flush with the boxes' front and back edges; if the unit will serve as a freestanding closet, the top should extend beyond the face of the boxes to hold a curtain rod.

Before assembling the parts, mark the locations of shelf-peg holes and drawer runners on the tall sides. Double check your measurements, then drill the ¼" peg holes. Cut the runners and fasten them in position, flush at front and back edges. Use two

flathead screws for each runner, countersinking the screw heads.

Assemble the parts at the spot where you will install the organizer. Glue and fasten the boxes with simple butt joints at the corners, as shown in the drawing, using 6d finishing nails. Set the nail heads and wipe off excess glue.

Mark closet-pole locations on the sides of the boxes, centering across the depth of the boxes, and screw their holders in place. Cut the closet poles and long shelves.

Fill nail holes and plywood edges; sand where needed. Paint with enamel.

Index

Boldface numbers refer to color photographs.

Adjustable beds, 7
Air beds, 16
Alcoves, 12, **27**, 32
Antiques, **30**, **43**, **53**, 74, **76**
    beds, 7–9
Architects, 12, 49
Armoire, **43**, 74
Art, **21**, **22**, 58, **61**
Atrium, 42, **43**
Attic bedrooms 5–6, **22**, **29**, **61**

Backrests, 23, **69**
Basement bedrooms, 5–6, **19**
Bathrooms, 6, **30**, 40–42, **43–46**, **52**, **76**, **78**
Bathtubs, 40–42, **43**, **46**
Bed
    frames, 7, 11–12, 47, 71
    placement, 12
    refinishing and repair, 7–9
    sizes, 10
    space-saving, 16–18, **19–22**
    types, 7–9
Bedside boxes, to build, 55
Bedside tables, to build, 31, 55
Bedspreads, 12, **28**, **35**, **38**, **45**, 50, **67**
Blinds, **27**, **43**, 50, **51**, **54**
Bookshelves, **22**, 26, **28–29**, **35**, **36–37**, 65, **67–68**
Box springs, 11
Brass beds, 8–9
Building codes, 18, 49
Bunkbeds, 16–17

Canopy beds, 9
Ceilings, 5, **28–30**, **35**, 50, **59**, **61**, **76**
Cheval glass, 74
Children's bedrooms, 6, 8, 16–17, 18
Closet, 24, 41, 42, **46**, 72–74, **75–78**, 79
Clothes storage, 72–74, **75–78**, 79
Corner-fitting headboard, 39, **61**, **68**
Curtains and draperies, **45**, 50, **75**
Cushions, 16, **38**

Day beds, 8, 17–18, **37**
Decks, 48–50, **51**, **54**
Designing, 12–13
Desks, **19**, 25, **27–30**

Doors
    bedroom offices, **30**
    closet, **27**, 73, **75–76**
    deck and patio, 49, **51**, **53**
    louver, **27**, **70**, 74
    small bedrooms, 15, **20–21**
Drawers, **19**, **27**, **29**, 44, **67–69**, 72–74, **75–78**
Drawings, 12–13
Dressing areas, 41, 72–74, **75–78**
Dumbwaiter, 6, 66

Electrical outlets, 64
Elevation drawings, 13
Energy conservation, 6, 33–34, 48–50, 56

Fireplaces, 33–34, **35**, **38**, **43**
Floor plans, 12–13
Foam mattresses, 10
Fold-away beds, 17
Fold-out beds, 16
Food and drink, 66
Furniture
    arrangement, 12–13, **21**, **28–29**, **35–38**, **68**
    to build, 23, 31, 39, 47, 55, 63, 71, 79
    built-ins, 14, 17–18, **19**, **20**, **22**, **27**, 33, **36**, **38**, **53**, **75–78**
    outside, 49–50, **51**
    seating, **22**, **29**, 32–33, **35–38**, **53**

Glass, **30**, 50, **51–54**
Guest rooms, 14–18, **19–22**, **37**

Hammocks, 18
Hanging beds, 18
Headboard cabinet, to build, 23
Headboards, 11–12, 15, 23, **29**, 39, **52**, **61**, **67–69**
Heat-circulating fireplaces, 34, **35**
Heating, 6, 34, 42, 48–49
Heat-recovery devices, 34
Hospital beds, 7
Hot tubs, 42, 49, **51**

Innerspring mattresses, 10–11
Interior designers, 12, 56
Interior windows, **21**, **22**, **30**, **53–54**

Japanese bed, 16, **21**

Lamps, 57–58
Light bridge, to build, 63
Lighting
    art, **61–62**
    basement, 5
    bedside, 57–58, **60–62**, **67**, **69**

Lighting (cont'd.)
    to build, 63
    ceiling, 57
    closet, 74
    dimmers, 56, 57
    energy-saving, 56
    fixtures, 56–58, **61**, **62**
    light bulbs, 56–58
    outdoor, **51**
    overall, 56–57, **59–61**
    planning, 56
    for special effects, **35**, 58, **59–62**
    task, 26
Lightwell, **54**, **68**
Linen press, 74
Linen storage, **38**, **70**, **76**
Location of bedrooms, 4–6
Loft bedrooms, 5–6, 18, **22**, **30**

Master bedroom suite, 5–6
Mattress bases, 11
Mattresses, 10–11
Metal beds, 8–9
Mirrors, 15, **20**, **43**, **44**, **46**, 56, 58, 73, 74, **75**, **77**, **78**
Multi-use bedrooms, 24–26, **27–30**, 32–34, **35–38**
Murphy bed, 17, **20**
Music, **37**, 65–66, **67**, **70**

Natural light, 26, 48–50, **51–54**, 74
Nurseries, 6

Offices in bedrooms, 5, **19**, 24–26, **27–30**, 49
Organizer, to build, 79
Out-of-doors, 48–50, **51–54**

Partitions
    bed and bath, 41, **43**, **52**
    bedroom offices, 25–26, **28–30**
    bedside amenities, **68–70**
    sitting areas, 32, **37**
    small bedrooms, **21**
    storage, **77**, **78**
Patios, 48–50, **51**, **53**
Pillow storage, **38**, **67**
Plans, 12–13
Plants, **44**, 49, **53**
Platform bed, to build, 47
Platform beds, 9, **19**, **29**, 33, 47, **53**, **67**
    pedestal-style, 9, **36**, 47, **54**, **67**
Plumbing, 41–42
Privacy, 4–5, 14, 18, 48–50

Sauna, 42
Second-story bedrooms, 5–6
Sewing in bedrooms, 24–26, **27–30**

Shades, **19–20**, 25–26, **30**, **38**, **43**, 50, **54**, **61**, **67**
Sheets, **22**, **69**
Shelves, 73–74
Shiki-buton, 16, **21**
Shower, 42
Sinks, 40–42, **45–46**
Site planning, 48–49
Sitting areas, 32–34, **35–38**
Skylights, **19**, **22**, **30**, **38**, **43–45**, 48–50, **51–52**, **54**, **76–78**
Slanting side tables, to build, 31
Sleeping environment, 48
Sleeping porch, 48
Small bedrooms, 14–18, **19–22**, **29**, **59**, **67**
Sofa beds, 16
Solar heating, 6, **35**, 48–50
Soundproofing, 25–26, 66
Sound systems, **37**, 65–66, **67**, **70**
Spa, 42
Stairs, 5–6, **22**, **30**
Storage
    bed frame, 71
    bedroom offices, 25, 26, **27**, **29**
    bedside boxes, 55
    clothes, 72–74, **75–78**, 79
    drawers under beds, **19**, **29**, **67**, **78**
    headboard, 23, **67**
    linen, **38**, **70**, **76**
    small bedrooms, 15
Sunlight, 48–50, **51–54**

Telephone, 64
Television, **22**, **37**, **54**, 64–65, **68**, **70**, **75**
Tile, 33, **35**, **38**, **43**, **46**, **68**
Traffic patterns, 13
Triangular headboard, to build, 39
Trundle beds, 16–17
Twin beds, 18

Utility porch, **19**

Ventilation, 5, 42, 49–50, 74
Vertical drapes (blinds), **68–69**, **77**
Vibrating beds, 9

Walk-in closets, 72, **75–78**
Wallpaper, **27**, **45**
Water bed frame, to build, 71
Water beds, 9–10, 71
Wicker furniture, 8
Windows, 48–50, **51–54**, 74
Window seats, 17–18, **22**, **38**, **44**
Wiring, 56–57, **67**
Wood stoves, 33–34, **37**
Workplace, 24–26, **27–30**

Photographers

Jack McDowell: front cover, 19 top, 20, 21, 22 top, 27, 35 bottom left & right, 37 bottom, 38 top left, 43 bottom, 45, 51 bottom, 53, 54 center, bottom left & right, 59, 60, 61, 62 bottom, 67 bottom, 68, 69 bottom, 70, 75, 76 bottom right, 77 top left & right. **Stephen W. Marley:** 22 bottom, 29 bottom right, 37 top, 51 top, 52, 62 top, 76 top left & right, 78 top left & right, bottom left. **Norman A. Plate:** 67 top. **Darrow M. Watt:** 19 bottom left & right, 22 center, 28, 29 top, bottom left, 30, 35 top, 36, 38 top right, bottom, 43 top, 44, 46, 54 top, 69 top, 77 bottom left, 78 bottom right, back cover.